# Quotes
# to Live By

Published in 2022 by The School of Life
First published in the USA in 2023
930 High Road, London, N12 9RT

Copyright © The School of Life 2022

Illustrations © Avi Ofer
Designed and typeset by Marcia Mihotich
Printed in Slovenia by DZS Grafik

A proportion of this book has appeared online at
www.theschooloflife.com/articles

Every effort has been made to contact the copyright holders of the
material reproduced in this book. If any have been inadvertently
overlooked, the publisher will be pleased to make restitution at the
earliest opportunity.

The School of Life publishes a range of books on essential topics in
psychological and emotional life, including relationships, parenting,
friendship, careers and fulfilment. The aim is always to help us
to understand ourselves better – and thereby to grow calmer, less
confused and more purposeful. Discover our full range of titles,
including books for children, here: www.theschooloflife.com/books

The School of Life also offers a comprehensive therapy service,
which complements, and draws upon, our published works:
www.theschooloflife.com/therapy

www.theschooloflife.com

ISBN 978-1-915087-04-1

10 9 8 7 6 5 4 3 2

# Quotes
# to Live By

The School of Life

# Introduction

Though we all tend to complain of being short of time, most of what we are served up to read is very long indeed. A dispiriting prejudice leads us collectively to associate length with depth – and brevity with shallowness. It would sound rather peculiar to claim that one's favourite work of literature might only be a couple of lines long.

But the history of thought is filled with masterpieces of concision. The art of the aphorism or maxim, though it has never been a dominant tradition, has enjoyed contributions from some of the greatest thinkers, including Seneca, La Rochefoucauld, Chamfort, Schopenhauer and Nietzsche.

A good aphorism removes everything extraneous to a thought so that it can travel with maximal ease, in its purest psychological essence and across gaps of culture, from one mind to another. Take the following aphorism:

'We all have strength enough to bear the misfortunes of others.'

Written in the aristocratic circles of mid-17th-century Paris by the Duc de La Rochefoucauld, it has carefully been shorn of any of the circumstances that gave rise to it; it has been polished into a hard gem-like form that is guaranteed to survive and spark recognition so long as humans are in existence. There might have been a particular lady with a castle in Burgundy, whose cloyingly pity-filled manner La Rochefoucauld especially wanted to skewer, and the thought might have come to him one night at the dinner table of the Baron X (where they were served veal and potato dauphinoise), but no such novelistic details are required. The thought escapes the setting that catalysed it and can find immediate application even in our own technological, secular times – as if La Rochefoucauld had personally known our aunt or overheard a conversation between two of our old friends.

Even if we have no pretensions to creating literature, trying to write aphorisms ourself can be of immense therapeutic value. We don't need to complain of any one set of people who might have annoyed us, or any one moment of special embarrassment or sorrow in our lives. We can recast the specific event in its general form. When we get home at night after another superficial social encounter or fretful day at the office, we can push ourselves to evaporate our travails into a cool, sharp-edged reflection that gives us a victory over the chaotic, troubling setting that laid the groundwork for it.

What follows is a collection of The School of Life's own aphorisms culled from across its emotional curriculum. The School of Life has always believed in the importance of not just attempting to say wise things but also of trying to make sure – with all the resources of art – that they can be noticed and have an effect on people at large. It does not trust that so long as our ideas are important, the style in which we deliver them is of no issue. Most of us are so distracted; if someone wants to get a point across, they must use extreme ingenuity to seize our attention and cauterise our boredom for a few moments. The School of Life imagines itself to be writing for an impatient audience with curious but restless minds.

The 17th-century French philosopher Pascal once famously apologised to a friend for writing him a long letter, explaining that he unfortunately had not had time to make it shorter. This touches teasingly on a sincere truth about aphorisms: they are a good deal more arduous to write than baggier pieces of prose. But the result – when it works – should be commensurately rewarding. Someone has produced a general rule out of a mere local instance of pain, joy or irritation – and gifted us a moment of clarity and solidarity. If the aphorisms contained here have correctly honoured their mission, it should be our lives we find repeatedly illuminated in the pages that follow; the book should know us as well as, and sometimes better than, we know ourselves.

# 1. Relationships

The only people we can think of as normal are those we don't yet know very well.

*

The challenge of marriage: we're at our most polite and humble with people when they are at their greatest liberty to leave us.

*

It is easiest to confidently seduce those we are least attracted to.

*

One can tell that an attraction has started when it becomes embarrassing to look at someone's wrists and, more so, their fingers.

*

All those unfair sounding complaints that your partner once reported their ex making against them, and to which you listened with so much sympathy on the early dates, you will – in time – end up understanding painfully well.

*

A silence with a beautiful person tends to leave you feeling you are the boring one.

*

It should count as a great psychological achievement to no longer automatically despise those who like us.

*

We keep imagining that we haven't met 'the right person'; we overlook that we might have the wrong picture of love.

*

Nature's exaggerated ways: to ensure that we will make, at most, four children in a lifetime, we have to desire obsessively from twelve to eighty.

*

There is as much sexual rejection within long-established relationships as there is among singles on the dating scene; it just hurts more.

*

Regret about exes: never trust what you feel now, only what you knew then.

*

In love, rather than being heralded as perfect, it is a great deal more reassuring, and therefore romantic, to be recognised as deeply flawed – but on that basis, deserving of boundless tenderness and patience.

*

One rarely falls in love without being as much attracted to what is interestingly wrong with someone as what is objectively healthy.

*

When we say that we want a partner with a good sense of humour, we don't want jokes in general; we want someone with the maturity to find themselves ridiculous. We're looking for an end to self-righteousness.

*

If we were properly sane, rather than being at once over-whelmed by the thought that we had found the one, we would calmly reflect: 'They seem nice enough and it will take twenty-five years to know more.'

*

It takes time and experience to realise that we cannot, in the end, rescue anyone – at best, just facilitate certain moves they were on their way to making anyway.

*

Serial philanderers have their own version of loyalty: loyalty to the emotions that accompany the start of love.

*

No wonder people are nervous on first dates: given what relationships typically entail, they should be terrified and mournful (especially if the date goes 'well').

*

Marriage ceremony: a couple making hopeful vows on behalf of two people whom they don't know – and who won't exist for another twenty years.

*

Love is a skill, not just an enthusiasm.

*

The partner best suited to us is not one who happens to share our every taste; it is the one who can negotiate differences in taste with intelligence and grace. Compatibility is an achievement of love; it shouldn't be its precondition.

*

The constant challenge of modern relationships: how to prove more interesting than the other's smartphone.

*

There is danger in those deeply insecure people who, entirely unconvinced of their own attractiveness, need to keep seducing new candidates to reassure themselves of their own charms.

*

It would be a foolhardy lover indeed who would want a completely honest answer to the anxious enquiry, 'What are you thinking about now?'

*

The only way to feel totally safe in someone else's love is to be shielded from much that courses through their mind.

*

Most relationship problems summed up: one person is standing too close; one person is standing too far away.

*

The best way to help a relationship is to not expect everything from relationships.

*

Ideally, we'd stop paying any attention at all to whether people tell us that they love us or not – and concentrate instead on whether or not they know how to be kind.

*

Choosing a spouse and choosing a career: the two great decisions for which society refuses to set up institutional guidance and that are – together – responsible for destroying more of our lives than all others.

*

People who are plain horrible are so much more survivable than those who mix in a bit of love with their trouble.

*

What can the most devoted lover offer us in terms of reassurance as compared with what was once natively on offer in the first home for which we unconsciously pine (the womb)?

*

In the midst of the biggest arguments in love, one is liable to appreciate deeply, and even want to sleep with, one's ostensible adversary.

*

There is nothing more romantic than to ask one's partner how one might inadvertently have angered or disappointed them – and then to listen non-defensively and modestly to whatever the answer might be for twenty minutes.

*

The fateful – and ungrateful – impulse to try to render inherently fugitive feelings of happiness permanent: to buy a house on the holiday island, to start the kind of business whose service we enjoyed, to marry the person we felt a rush of love for.

*

We seldom say starkly vicious things to people unless we love them a lot; it's a sign of immense hope that has been shaken. In our fury, what we may be trying to say is: 'I'm scared that I love you so much and that you can rattle me so easily.' It's an unfortunate paradox of the human brain that such an emotion can come out as: 'I wish you were dead.'

*

To consider another with love means forever remembering the child within them. Our wrongdoer may be fully grown, but their behaviour is necessarily poignantly connected up with their early years.

*

We're so keen never to patronise people by treating them as younger than they are that we overlook the need to occasionally ignore their outward adult sides in order to honour and sympathise with the angry or hurt infant lurking inside.

*

A sibling is to a childhood what an adulterous lover is to a marriage: not good news – and, as always with things that aren't good news, the best way to handle things is to allow people to admit, with utter directness, how awful they really are.

*

When we are around small children who frustrate us, we don't declare them evil; we find less alarming ways of interpreting the origins of their difficult behaviour: perhaps they are getting a bit tired, their gums are sore or they are upset by the arrival of a younger sibling. Given how immature every adult necessarily remains, the moves we execute with relative ease around children must forever continue to be relevant when dealing with another so-called grown-up.

*

Marriage isn't a vow to stop being interested in other people; it's a commitment as to how to handle that interest.

*

It may sound kind but we are doing a partner, and ourselves, a proper disservice when we promise we will never leave them. There is nothing more likely to usher in the death of love than the whispered words 'I *will always be with you*.' It isn't fair to expect anyone to appreciate what they are never able to fear losing.

*

It takes a great deal of maturity to be able to tolerate a partner who threatens to be reliably nice to us.

*

We are more often 'good', not so much from any intrinsic virtue as from a lack of opportunity for transgression.

*

Where we find an attention-seeking partner, an attention-denying partner isn't generally far behind.

*

We keep a special place in our hearts for people who refuse to be impressed by us.

*

Few events have the power to alter priorities as swiftly and decisively as an orgasm.

*

Sexual liberation appeals mostly to people who haven't got anything too destructive or weird they long to satisfy once they've been liberated.

*

The fastest technique for messing up one's life remains that of getting into a serious relationship with the wrong person: with very little effort, and without any innate taste for catastrophe, one can end up – by middle age or earlier – contemplating wholesale financial ruin, loss of parental rights, social opprobrium, homelessness, nervous exhaustion and shattered esteem, to begin a lengthy list of harrowing side-effects. It may be rather fun and, in a way, sweet to watch couples on their early dates, in their fine garb, downing cocktails while outside on a mild summer evening, boats sail by and music drifts in. But it's like witnessing a toddler playing with a loaded rifle or ceramic steak knife.

*

A bond between two people can be deep and important precisely because it is not played out across all practical details of existence. By simplifying – and clarifying – what a relationship is for, we release ourselves from overly complicated conflicts – and focus on our urgent underlying needs to be sympathised with, seen and understood.

*

The best way to make a relationship last is to limit what we expect it to be about. We might not socialise much together. We might hardly ever encounter each other's families. Our finances might overlap only at a few points. We could be living in different places and only meet up twice a week. Conceivably, we might not even ask too many questions about each other's sex life. But when we would be together, it would be profoundly gratifying, because we would be in the presence of someone ultimately kind, vulnerable and understanding.

*

The single greatest predictor of ending up in an unhappy adult relationship is, in a phenomenon that layers misery upon misery, simply and squarely the extent to which we have had a miserable time at the hands of significant others in our early lives.

*

It is expecting too much to think that we might have been substantially unloved as children and then grow up to easily make reasonable choices as to our partners in our adult years. The best we could aim for is a live appreciation that our instincts are liable to be profoundly unreliable guides to our needs.

*

Intimacy: the capacity to be rather weird with someone – and the discovery that that's OK with them.

*

The point of marriage is not so much to be in love as to stop having to think of love.

*

A troubled past gives us a touching but ultimately disastrous tendency to think against ourselves – and so to give an unnatural degree of credit to troubling partners.

*

A difficult past will make us unusually unforgiving towards genuine kindness when it comes along. We may be unable to quite put a finger on what feels wrong with our very kind date. We might say there was no chemistry or that our interests didn't align. But if we knew ourselves better, what we would express would sound a lot stranger: that certain candidates felt wrong because we sensed they would be unlikely to be able to torture us in the way we require to experience love.

*

We can get better at daring to ask people out on a date when we grasp that we're not thereby asking them what we unconsciously think we're asking: 'Do I deserve to exist?' We're asking something far more innocent, and far more survivable were the answer to be negative: 'Might you be free on Friday?'

*

Anyone can land on a disturbed partner; the healthy among us can be identified by the speed with which they assess the problem and the decisiveness and deftness with which they can exit.

*

We should beware of any partner who, when one politely levels a complaint against them, takes offence rather than grows curious.

*

The complaint of people that they 'haven't been heard' instantly draws sympathy. But it might also mask that they haven't had the courage to express themselves clearly.

*

Few things inspire more insight and creativity than people who profoundly disappoint us; we should (almost) offer them thanks.

*

The cruelty of unrequited love isn't really that we haven't been loved back, but that our hopes have been aroused by someone who can never disappoint us, and that we will have to keep believing in because we lack the knowledge that would set us free.

*

Untrustworthy people are always berating us 'to trust more' – rather than working on offering us genuine reasons to do so.

∗

We are so impressed by honesty, we have forgotten the virtues of politeness – this word defined not as a cynical withholding of important information for the sake of harm but as a dedication to not rubbing someone else up against the hurtful aspects of the truth.

∗

It is ultimately no great sign of kindness to insist on showing someone our entire selves at all times. Repression, a certain degree of restraint and a dedication to editing our pronouncements belong to love as much as a capacity for explicit confession.

∗

The person who cannot tolerate secrets, who, in the name of 'being honest', divulges information so wounding it cannot be forgotten, is no friend of love.

∗

People reveal their sanity by their gracious knowledge and acceptance of their mad sides. A standard question on any initial dinner date should simply be: 'In what particular ways are you crazy?' We should beware of those who can't answer or get offended.

*

An epidemic of loneliness has been generated by the misguided idea that the only alternative to feeling alone is to be in a romantic relationship.

*

We are ready for love when we can accept that everyone we could get together with would be trouble in some very substantial ways.

*

When a lie is told in a relationship, we can blame the liar for sure, but we should also examine if the bar for honesty was not set too high.

*

Given what the institution normally entails, to ask someone we care for to marry us seems the height of disrespect, cruelty and paradox.

*

The most dangerous people to try to get together with: those labouring under the illusion that they might be easy to live with.

*

To show ourselves 'as we truly are' – a terrifying treat we should spare most of humanity and, in particular, anyone we claim to love.

*

We shouldn't simply blame the other person for their faults; we should recognise that we were positively once attracted to such 'faults' – because we were seeking to recreate a pattern of non-fulfilment we knew in childhood.

*

We generally search in relationships not for what is going to be most pleasurable but for what will feel most familiar. To know this is to feel compassion for ourselves and forgiveness for the partner: how could they have known that we wanted them in part because they would frustrate us?

*

We must be civilised and grown up with everyone else, but with one person on the planet, we can, at points, be maddeningly irrational, utterly demanding and horribly cross – not because they deserve it but because so much has gone wrong for us in other areas; we are so tired, and they are the one person who promises to understand and forgive us. No wonder we love them.

*

The capacity to compromise is not always the weakness it is described as being. It can involve a mature, realistic admission that there may – in certain situations – simply be no ideal options. And, conversely, an inability to compromise does not always have to be courageous and visionary; it may just be a rigid and proud delusion.

*

Wiser societies would be careful never to stigmatise the act of compromise. It is painful enough to have to compromise; it is even more painful to have to hate oneself for having done so. We should rehabilitate and honour the ability to put up with a flawed fellow human being, to nurse our sadness without falling into rage or despair, to reconcile ourselves to our damaged appearance and character and to accept that there may be no better way for us to live but partly in pain and longing, given who we are and what the world can provide. Couples who compromise may, in reality, not be the enemies of love; they may be at the vanguard of understanding what lasting relationships truly demand.

*

It is friendship that often offers us the real route to the pleasures that Romanticism associates with love. In a better world, our most serious goal would not be to locate one special lover with whom to replace all other humans, but to put our intelligence and energy into identifying and nurturing a circle of true friends. At the end of an evening, we would learn to say to certain prospective companions, with an embarrassed smile as we invited them inside – knowing that this would come across as a properly painful rejection – 'I'm so sorry. Couldn't we just be ... lovers?'

\*

A good partnership is not so much one between two healthy people (there aren't many of these on the planet); it's one between two people who have had the skill or luck to find a non-threatening accommodation between their relative insanities, in large part because they have a good grasp of how ill and difficult to live with they are.

\*

We should create room for regular moments, perhaps as often as every few hours, when we can feel unembarrassed and legitimate about asking for confirmation of the other's ongoing affection. 'I really need you; do you still want me?' should be the most normal of enquiries. We should uncouple the admission of need from any associations with the unfortunate and punitive term 'neediness'.

*

We do our fellow adults the greatest possible favour when we are able to regard at least some of their bad behaviour as we would that of an infant. We are so wary of belittling, we forget that it is also, at times, the greatest privilege for someone to look beyond our adult self in order to engage with – and forgive – the disappointed, furious, inarticulate or wounded child within.

*

In relationships, we're not properly home from a trip alone just when we walk in the door, but only after we've had (and resolved) the first big argument generated by our absence.

*

It is a privilege to be the recipient of a sulk, for one only tends to fall into a sulk with people whom one feels should understand one, in whom one has placed a high degree of trust – and yet who appear to have broken the contract of the relationship. We would never dare to storm out of a room, call someone a shit and stay silent the rest of the evening in an upstairs room unless we were with a partner whom we, in the background, believed had a profound capacity to understand us, which they had – strangely, probably out of spite – chosen not to use on this occasion. A sulk is one of the stranger gifts of love.

*

The two things we try so hard never to communicate directly to our partners in love: 'I need you' and 'You have hurt me'. We'll go to any lengths to act out our pain rather than spell out our vulnerability.

*

Some of us need to learn that there are people who just don't change: their characters have been bolted shut through trauma and there is no chance that they will ever – whatever they may say and promise – display any evolution. We may need to do something very strange: walk away. This is not a sign of cowardice or weakness of character, just a symptom that we have (finally) learnt to love ourselves enough to place our needs more firmly at the centre of our considerations.

*

If the school curriculum were shaped by a subject's contribution to our chances of future happiness, at least half of classes would be on relationships.

*

The illusion of having an easy-going nature is a privilege granted only to those who live on their own.

*

It's a sad day when couples start to complain about one another, but an infinitely sadder one when they no longer bother.

*

The more we listen to children, the less hard they have to scream. A child who says they want to burn the school down doesn't want to burn the school down; they want to be heard for the deep frustration that school is causing them. They will only become an arsonist if we continue to shut our ears.

\*

The greatest contribution to children's welfare is the removal of the idea that everyone should have children. A truly child-focused society would give equal prestige to childless and childful states.

\*

We best honour children, the born and the unborn, by accepting that parenting should never be the automatic choice – just as the wisest way to ensure that people will have happy marriages is to destigmatise singlehood.

\*

Some of the best people in existence do not make ideal parents; the truly great ones know this about themselves and act bravely on the knowledge.

\*

The world is never unhappy because of children who have not yet been born; it is grief-stricken by children who have been placed on the planet without anyone to love them adequately. We can cope with fewer children; we can't cope with yet more parents insufficiently dedicated to the tasks of love.

*

The good-enough parent feels sufficiently resourceful inside itself not to hold it against the child that it is making a very big deal out of so-called 'nothing'. It will follow the child in its excitement over a puddle and in its grief over an uncomfortable sock. It understands that the child's future ability to be considerate to other people and to handle genuine disasters will be critically dependent on having had its ample fill of sympathy for a range of age-appropriate sorrows.

*

The good parent knows that children may well cling for a long while and will never dismiss this natural need for reassurance in pejorative terms. It won't tell the child to 'buck up' and be a 'good little man' or 'young lady who can make me proud'. It will know that those who end up securely attached and able to tolerate absence are those who were originally allowed to have as much dependence and connection as they needed. There will be few requests to be 'brave' at the school gates.

*

The more capable a child is of surviving without its parents, the more he or she is at liberty to find them annoying.

*

On 'privileged' childhoods: true privilege is an emotional phenomenon. It involves receiving the nectar of love – which can be stubbornly missing in the best equipped mansions and oddly abundant in the bare rooms of modest bungalows.

*

Humbling parental realisation at adolescence: that, despite the angelic flutterings of the early years, we have, in the end, only brought another human being into the world.

*

## 2. Self-Knowledge

A feeling that one might really be quite a 'nice person': a sure sign that one hasn't begun to understand oneself.

\*

Going a bit mad for a time is a very common and ultimately rather sane rite of passage.

\*

'Just be yourself' is about the worst advice one can give some people.

\*

Maturity: the confidence to have no opinions on many things.

\*

The good parent: someone who can bear, for a time, over certain important things, to be hated by their offspring.

\*

We're all geniuses deep inside, just with a greater – or a lesser – capacity to get the good ideas out.

\*

Much of life is about correctly determining on whom and on what we should finally give up.

*

The chief benefit of being an imperfect parent: your children will one day want to leave home and try to do better.

*

Hypochondria: an imaginative response to the deeply improbable nature of being and remaining alive.

*

We're taught to be suspicious of self-help. It has its vainglorious aspects when one is being helped to flatten one's stomach or make a fortune. It reaches its true promise when one is being dissuaded from killing oneself.

*

Most of what we try so hard to hide from others is immediately obvious to the first stranger.

*

Feeling one is broadly leading the right life is entirely compatible with being grumpy most of the time.

*

It's the height of immaturity to strongly resent sometimes being treated as a child.

*

'We're determined not to let the birth of our first disrupt our lives too much.' It's important to keep a completely straight face at this point.

*

Pain shrinks time horizons; in extreme crises, we concentrate on the next minute going well.

*

If we let the impact of events and encounters truly resonate, we would need hours to process minutes.

*

We grow kinder the more our own lives grow susceptible to unkind interpretations.

*

It's so normal to want a better life; it's so unusual to set out to be a better person.

*

Rather than feel guilt, people who have hurt us typically start to hate us – for reminding them of their cruelty.

*

Long before they are political beliefs, right and left are emotional dispositions.

*

When one is finally feeling lucid, clear-eyed and rational, people often ask if one might be drunk.

*

As adults, we strive to cultivate the character traits that might have rescued our parents.

*

Definition of a parent: an ordinary human whose significance – kindness, evil, guilt, credit – is impossible not to exaggerate.

*

The largest part of what we call 'personality' is determined by how we have opted to defend ourselves against anxiety and sadness.

*

We should aim to have a better grasp of our own awful sides than our worst enemy ever could.

*

It takes a profound lack of imagination to have an entirely clean conscience.

*

It isn't logical that 'being happy' should be any easier than learning the violin – or require any less effort.

*

Most of our childhood is stored not in photos, but in certain biscuits, lights of day, smells, textures of carpet.

*

A goal of parenting: to make offspring feel so special for a time, they'll later have the strength to acknowledge and make their peace with their true insignificance.

*

A parent who fails is giving a child a gift of sorts. They allow them to discover that failure is part of every life. They're offering their child something more important than an unblemished childhood: a sincere one and an induction in how to approach their own darker sides, which they will come across soon enough. By being perfect, a parent is not being perfect; they're making the child feel ashamed of their flawed humanity.

*

'To be honest ...' – a prefix that hints at a last vain stab of conscience before a great untruth.

*

A 'boring person' is merely someone lacking the courage to be sufficiently in touch with the more troubled visceral parts of themselves.

*

Good thinking demands periods when we have no idea what other people are thinking.

*

There are two ways to keep a population passive: give them so little news, no one knows what is going on. Or deluge them with so much news, no one can keep track of what matters.

*

Bitterness: anger that forgot where it came from.

*

The true test of moral character: how we treat people who can do nothing for us.

*

The craving to be liked by people who we don't like should be treated as a neurosis like any other.

*

It's always tempting to find others 'a bit thin skinned' in coping with our rudeness, egoism and insensitivity.

*

How we respond to the insistent wailing of a small child reveals a lot about what the world has done to our dreams.

*

Love your children reliably and they'll outgrow you. Ignore them and they'll be obsessed with you for life.

*

Some of our greatest insights come when we stop trying to be purposeful and instead respect the creative potential of daydreaming, that strategic rebellion against the excessive demands of immediate pressures, in favour of the diffuse, earnest exploration of our convoluted deep selves.

*

A central task of culture is to remind us that the laws of nature apply to us as well as to trees, animals and the planets. Our goal is to get clearer about where our own tantalisingly powerful yet always limited agency stops – and where we will be left with no option but to bow to forces infinitely greater than our own.

*

A sneaking respect for children who burst into tears when a fork is not exactly in the right place: how much we have to abandon our own exacting standards.

*

We expend so much hope and energy on solving one-off worries, forgetting the darker truth that we may, in the end, just be perennially anxious people, perpetually re-placing one topic of alarm for another – and always in search of something to cloud our mood.

*

Being worried may, in the end, just feel far more normal – and therefore relaxing.

*

Our vulnerability to simple psychological errors is no more absurd, and no less poignant, than the idea that an adult can be killed by a well-aimed pebble or that we can die for want of a glass of water.

*

Anxiety deserves greater dignity. It is not a sign of degeneracy; it is a justifiable expression of panic at our mysterious participation in a disordered, uncertain world.

∗

Anxiety is insight that we haven't yet found a productive use for, that hasn't yet made its way into an idea.

∗

We can do most of our best work in our sleep, so long as we know what questions to ask ourselves before losing consciousness.

∗

We make our lives tougher than they should be because we insist on thinking of people, ourselves and others as inept and mean rather than, as is almost invariably the case, primarily the victims of what we have all in some way travelled through: an immensely tricky early history.

∗

Jolliness sounds almost indistinguishable from happiness. But with its remorseless and insistent quality, aggressive jolliness has very little to do with true satisfaction. The jollier doesn't just want the mood to be happy; they can't tolerate that it might in any way be sad – so unexplored and potentially overwhelming are their own background feelings of disappointment and grief.

*

A defence of self-knowledge has nothing to do with high-minded morality. It is ultimately cautionary. We need to tell ourselves a little more of our own truth because we pay too high a price for our concealments. We cut ourselves off from possibilities of growth. We shut off large portions of our minds and end up uncreative, tetchy and defensive, while others around us have to suffer our irritability, gloom, manufactured cheerfulness and defensive rationalisations.

*

We may think of egoists as people who have grown sick from too much love. But the opposite is always the case: an egoist is someone who has not yet had their fill. Self-centeredness has to have a clean run in the early years, if it isn't to haunt and ruin the later ones. The so-called narcissist is simply a benighted soul who has not had a chance to be inordinately and unreasonably admired and cared for at the start.

*

We take the first steps towards maturity by determining some of the ways in which our emotional minds deny, lie, evade, forget, obsess and steer us towards goals that won't deliver the satisfaction of which we're initially convinced. A readiness to mitigate the worst of our everyday foolishness contributes to the highest kind of emotional intelligence of which we may ever be capable.

*

When they suffer at the hands of an adult, children almost invariably take what happens to them as a reflection of something that must be very wrong with *them*.

*

Maturity involves accepting with good grace that we are all – like marionettes – manipulated by the past. And, when we can manage it, that we should therefore develop our capacity to judge and act in the here and now with somewhat greater fairness and neutrality.

*

It is a sign of our lack of civilisation that we insist on thinking of baths primarily as tools to clean ourselves with, rather than honouring them as what they truly are: instruments of mental health. Those of us who suffer in our minds should not be embarrassed to have multiple baths a day. They will be the enamel ships that carry us over the worst of our griefs.

*

One of the great contributing factors to mental illness is the idea that we should be well at all costs and all times. We suffer far more than we should because of how long it can take many of us until we allow ourselves to fall properly and usefully ill.

*

We should learn from physical rehabilitation how long it might take to feel well again. Recovery from a broken wrist might take six months, and it can be a year before a new hip is functioning once more. A mind that's broken can take longer still – it could be one or two years, even four or five. We shouldn't be surprised: the mind is a far more complex organ than any bone or muscle and so warrants a correspondingly lengthy period of recuperation.

＊

Anyone who has ever suffered from mental illness and who recovers will do so because of an experience of love, whether they consciously realise it or not. By extension, no one has ever fallen gravely mentally ill without – somewhere along the line – having suffered from a severe deficit of love. Love turns out to be the guiding strand running through the onset of, and recovery from, our worst episodes of mental unwellness.

＊

We may have become experts over many years in the language of illness and self-torture. It will take a great deal of time to become fluent in the language of generosity and self-compassion.

*

A breakdown is not merely a random piece of madness or malfunction; it can be a very real – albeit inarticulate and inconvenient – bid for health. It is an attempt by one part of our minds to force the other into a process of growth, self-understanding and self-development, which it has hitherto been too cowed to undertake. If we can put it paradoxically, it is an attempt to jumpstart a process of getting well, properly well, through a stage of falling very ill.

*

We shouldn't be so surprised at the enormous levels of mental illness at large in society; we need only get clear how bad we collectively are at love, how poor we are at lending sympathy, at listening, at offering reassurance, at feeling compassion and at forgiving – and, conversely, how good we are at hating, shaming and neglecting.

*

While thinking through our problems is crucial to our health, to attempt to think without enough sleep is worse than not thinking at all. The thinking we do when tired is vindictive and sloppy. It misses important details; it gives the advantage over to our enemies; it hands victory to the evangelists of sadness. It isn't a disrespect to the power of the mind to insist that we should not attempt to fire up this machine unless and until it has been adequately well rested – like a powerful rocket or an exquisite motorboat that we wouldn't dare to activate unless we could be sure of a clear sky or a calm sea.

*

We should never take seriously any worry that suddenly appears extremely pressing after midnight. What we panic about in the early hours should automatically be discounted. We should accept that night destroys reason.

*

A categorical fact of psychological life is the disinclination of any child to think that there is something wrong with its parent, even when there very much is; it will go to almost any lengths to prevent the idea emerging that its parent may be mentally unwell or fundamentally brutish. It will remain attached and obsessed by the most vicious and uncaring figure whom an objective observer would see through in an instant. It prefers to hate itself rather than get angry with those who have let it down.

*

Small children naturally turn injury done to them into dislike of themselves. They ask not so much, 'Why does my parent fail to care for me?' as, 'How might I have failed this admirable person?' They hate themselves rather than doubting those who should be protecting them; shame replaces anger. It feels, on balance, like the safer option.

*

The leading symptom of having been traumatised is fear of the future. Traumatised people are, above anything else, scared of what is to come. The psychoanalyst Donald Winnicott observed: 'The catastrophe you fear *will* happen has *already happened*.' That is why, in order to find out the gist of what might have occurred to us long ago, we should ask ourselves not so much about the past (we won't directly be able to remember) but about what we are afraid will happen to us going forward. Our apprehension holds the clues to our history.

*

Traumatised people don't go around thinking that they are unnaturally scared; they just think that everything is terrifying. They don't notice their appallingly low sense of self-worth; they just assume that others are likely to mock and dislike them. They don't realise how uncomfortable intimacy is; they merely report not being happy in this or that relationship. In other words, trauma colours our view of reality but at the same time, prevents us from noticing the extent to which we are peering at life through distorted lenses.

*

People who have grown up not to like themselves very much at all have an above average risk of suffering from extremes of anxiety, for if one doesn't think one is worthy, it must – by a dastardly logic – follow that the world is permanently and imminently at high risk of punishing one in the way one suspects one deserves.

\*

For the self-hating, anxiety is a pre-emptive anticipation of the pain one unconsciously feels one is owed; very bad things must and should happen to very bad people.

\*

We are utterly reliant on an inner sense of having been valued inordinately by another person at the start as a protection against the subsequent neglect of the world. We don't need to be loved by many; one will do, and twelve years might be enough, sixteen ideally. But without this, the eternal admiration of millions won't ever be able to convince us of our goodness. And with love, the scorn of millions won't ever need to be fatal.

\*

The emotionally deprived return, almost manically to the question, never really settled, of 'Do I deserve to exist?' And this is why they typically put unusual effort into attempts to be famous and visibly successful. It would seldom occur to anyone who has been properly loved to be known to strangers.

\*

Paranoia is the masked return of childhood-induced shame at one's own being.

\*

In the midst of a breakdown, we often wonder whether we have gone mad. We have not. We're behaving oddly no doubt, but beneath the surface agitation, we are on a hidden yet logical search for health. We haven't become ill; we were ill already. Our crisis is an attempt to dislodge us from a demented status quo and an insistent call to rebuild our lives on a more authentic and sincere basis.

\*

There is no maturity without an adequate negotiation with the infantile and no such thing as a proper grown-up who is not frequently visited by all the emotions of a toddler.

*

Our democratic instincts show up in a strong tendency to assume that the broad consensus of our society must always and invariably be pretty much right on all matters. We should do ourselves the honour of accepting, at moments, that most people might – over many things – be very wrong.

*

We crave the validation of others in inverse proportion to how well we think of ourselves. If we could truly accept ourselves as decent, public opinion would be of no interest whatsoever.

*

Somewhere in childhood, our trajectory towards emotional maturity will have been impeded. Even if we were sensitively cared for and lovingly handled, we can be counted upon not to have passed through our young years without sustaining a great many habits of mind that make us less than perfectly lucid, balanced and easy to interact with.

*

Our sad moods strongly imply that they are about what lies ahead of us, but very often, they exist chiefly as symptoms of a difficult past; they stem from a projected memory of people around us who once told us, with particular authority, that we were no good, that we would fail, that we should be ashamed of ourselves and that catastrophe was around the corner. We should learn to historicise such voices and differentiate them from a trustworthy verdict on the present. Our low moods are far more about a past we still need fully to mourn than a future there is any reason to dread.

*

We shouldn't be tough on ourselves for lingering so long in a school-based 'others know best' mindset. School is an immensely impressive system. We start there when we are not much bigger than a chair. For more than a decade, it's all we know; it is the outside world – and what those who love us most tell us we should respect. It speaks with immense authority, not just about itself but about life in general. It is sold to us as a preparation for the whole of existence. But, of course, the main thing it does is to prepare us for yet more school; it is an education in how to thrive within its own profoundly peculiar rules – with only a tenuous connection to the world beyond. Knowing all this, we might do a very strange-sounding thing: finally work up the courage to leave our inner school – be it at twenty-eight, thirty-five or sixty-two – and enter the wider boundless world we have been in flight from for too long.

*

Being defensive does not spring from arrogance or pride. It is the adult relic of a childhood fear of what could happen if a mistake were to be admitted – projected into situations where such risks no longer apply.

*

The timid tend to live – paradoxically – in terror of being accused of boasting. So whatever good they have accomplished, they take great care to hide. If something has gone well, they publicly put it down to luck and privately assume that far worse is soon to come. But there might be an opportunity, every now and then, to acknowledge what has been a success. One might try, on occasion, to stop putting oneself down and open up about a success one has been involved in. It could feel as dangerous as shoplifting, yet maturity may mean finally daring to take the measure of, and a little pride in, one's own virtues.

*

Whatever the risks of overlooking others' uniqueness, there is an equal risk in believing too strongly in our own singularity. On occasion, we should tread across the perceived gulf that separates us from the rest of humanity and simply guess that, probably, the other person is as bored as we are, or would quite like to have a laugh as much as we do, or that they are as nervous as we have been – or as much in need of a friend.

*

The full grandeur and seriousness of the concept of adolescence is too often obscured by its association with grumpiness and acne. But something very serious is being trialled out in this phase: permission to complain. Many of us, unknown to ourselves, managed not to have an adolescence at fifteen. There wasn't enough love to dare to. Not every parent is mature enough to allow themselves to be hated and belittled. We may be close to menopause or past retirement before we have the courage finally to question whether we really always have to obey and forgive.

*

The true crime isn't to have succeeded; it's to have been brought up to associate one's success with arrogance.

*

We are used to taking our fears as reliable alarm bells. If we don't want to go to the party, it must be because gatherings are dangerous. If we don't want to start a new initiative, it must be because the risk is untenable. But some alarms may be going off for no good reason at all, simply because we've grown up feeling suspicious of ourselves. Fear, which is, in principle, there to help us take care of our interests, may be shielding us from being properly alive. We might – at selected points – need to hear an alarm, acknowledge its force – and walk right on.

*

Children who grow up in the company of difficult adults settle on doing one thing extremely well: hoping against hope that these adults will magically change and learn to be kind. If they just hold on long enough, and are sufficiently polite and compliant, then the difficult adult will take mercy and alter. These suffering souls then take their misguided patience out into their adult relationships, with similarly negligible results. They are barred from a crucial insight: that health, at points, involves a lively capacity for giving up on certain people.

*

We suffer from ideas of what should be normal that aren't normal.

*

Almost everything we are today is the result of patterns laid down in childhood that we have forgotten. Children are not constitutionally made to understand their own psychology. They can tell you about distant planets way before they have any grasp of their motives or emotions. The first ten years were blind. We now have to go back and re-interpret them.

*

Our chance of leading a fulfilled adult life depends over-whelmingly on our knowledge of, and engagement with, the nature of our childhood.

*

It's an inbuilt preference of the mind to be gloomy in general rather than sad about certain things in particular.

*

The most troubled people will always have a more than average attachment to the idea that they are sane.

*

Without a proper understanding of childhood, it won't matter how many fortunes we have made, how stellar our reputation or outwardly cheerful our families, we will be doomed to founder on our own psychological complexities; we will be sunk by anxiety, lack of trust, dread, paranoia, rage and self-loathing – those legacies of distorted and misunderstood pasts.

*

There are, on the surface, some notable similarities between those who are sad and those who are depressed. Both groups cry; both withdraw from the world; both complain of listlessness and a sense of alienation from their normal lives. But there is one categorical difference between depression and sadness: *the sad person knows what they are sad about; the depressed person doesn't.*

*

The depressed person isn't depressed – as they might suggest – *for no reason.* They are very distressed about something but that something is proving extremely difficult to take on board, and has therefore been pushed into the outer zones of consciousness – from where it wreaks havoc on the whole person, prompting boundless feelings of nihilism. Depressives unconsciously choose to remain dead to everything, as opposed to very distraught about something. Depression is sadness that has forgotten its true causes.

*

The desire to be good is one of the loveliest things in the world, but in order to have a genuinely good life, we may sometimes need to be (by the standards of the people pleaser we might be) fruitfully and bravely 'bad'.

*

When we eat too much, often the cause of the problem isn't an unconstrained appetite; it is our difficulty in getting access to the psychological nutrients that could feed our broken souls – understanding, tenderness, forgiveness, reconciliation and closeness. We can eat too much, not because we are (as we brutally accuse ourselves) greedy but because the emotional ingredients we crave are so elusive.

*

A pessimist is someone who calmly assumes from the outset, and with a great deal of justification, that things tend to turn out really very badly in almost all areas of existence. Strange though it can sound, pessimism is one of the greatest sources of serenity, wry humour and contentment.

*

Like optimists, pessimists would like things to go well. But by recognising that many things can – and probably will – go wrong, the pessimist is better placed to secure the good outcome both parties ultimately seek. Having never expected anything to go right, the pessimist tends to end up with one or two things to smile about.

*

It can feel like an insult to our rational adult dignity to think that our sense of gloom might in the end stem, centrally, from exhaustion or low blood sugar. We'd sooner identify ourselves as up against an existential crisis than see ourselves as sleep-deprived or missing an orange juice.

*

Probably as a hangover from childhood, 'staying up late' feels a little glamorous and even exciting; late at night is when (in theory) the most fascinating things happen. But in a wiser culture than our own, some of the most revered people in the land would – on a regular basis – be shown taking to bed early. There'd be competitions highlighting sensible bedtimes. We'd be reminded of the pleasures of already being in bed when the last of the evening light still lingers in the sky. Our problems would not thereby disappear, but our strength to confront them would, at points, critically increase.

*

The wise are 'realistic' about how challenging many things can be. They are fully conscious of the complexities entailed in any project – for example, raising a child, starting a business, spending an agreeable weekend with the family, changing the nation, falling in love ... Knowing that something difficult is being attempted doesn't rob the wise of ambition, but it makes them more steadfast, calmer and less prone to panic about the problems that will invariably come their way. The wise rarely expect anything to be wholly easy or to go entirely well.

*

Properly aware that much can and will go wrong, the wise are unusually alive to moments of calm and beauty, even extremely modest ones, of the kind that those with grander plans rush past. With the dangers and tragedies of existence firmly in mind, they can take pleasure in a single uneventful sunny day, or some pretty flowers growing by a brick wall, the charm of a three-year-old playing in a garden or an evening of intimate conversation among friends. It isn't that they are sentimental and naive; it's precisely the opposite: because they have seen how hard things can get, they know how to draw the full value from the peaceful and the sweet – whenever and wherever these arise.

\*

The wise know that all human beings, themselves in-cluded, are never far from folly: they have irrational de-sires and incompatible aims; they are unaware of a lot of what they feel; they are prone to mood swings; they are visited by powerful fantasies and delusions – and are always buffeted by the curious demands of their sexuali-ty. The wise are unsurprised by the ongoing co-existence of deep immaturity and perversity alongside quite adult qualities like intelligence and morality. They know that we are barely evolved apes. Aware that at least half of life is irrational, they try – wherever possible – to budget for madness and are slow to panic when it (reliably) rears its head.

*

The wise take the business of laughing at themselves seriously. They hedge their pronouncements; they are sceptical in their conclusions. Their certainties are not as brittle as those of others. They laugh from the con-stant collisions between the noble way they'd like things to be and the demented way they in fact often turn out.

*

The wise are realistic about social relations, in particular, about how difficult it is to change people's minds and have an effect on their lives. They are, therefore, extremely reticent about telling others too frankly what they think. They have a sense of how seldom it is useful to get censorious with others. They want – above all – to be nice in social settings, even if this means they are not totally authentic. So they will sit with someone of an opposite political persuasion and not try to convert them; they will hold their tongue at someone who seems to be announcing a wrong-headed plan for reforming the country, educating their child or directing their personal life. They'll be aware of how differently things can look through the eyes of others and will search more for what people have in common than what separates them.

\*

The wise have made their peace with the yawning gap between how they would ideally want to be and what they are actually like. They have come to terms with their tendencies to idiocy, ugliness and error. They are not fundamentally ashamed of themselves, because they have already shed so much of their pride.

\*

The wise are realistic about other people. They recognise the extraordinary pressures everyone is under to pursue their own ambitions, defend their interests and seek their own pleasures. It can make others appear extremely 'mean' and purposefully evil, but this would be to over-personalise the issue. The wise know that most hurt is not intentional; it's a by-product of the constant collision of blind competing egos in a world of scarce resources. The wise are therefore slow to anger and judge. They don't leap to the worst conclusions about what is going on in the minds of others. They will be readier to overlook a hurt from a proper sense of how difficult every life is, harbouring as it does so many frustrated ambitions, disappointments and longings. The wise appreciate the pressures people are under. Of course they shouted; of course they were rude; naturally they want to appear as slightly more important ... The wise are generous to the reasons for which people might not be nice. They feel less persecuted by the aggression and meanness of others, because they have a sense of where it comes from: a place of hurt.

*

The wise have a solid sense of what they can survive. They know just how much can go wrong and things will still be – just about – liveable. The unwise person draws the boundaries of their contentment much too far out, so that it encompasses, and depends upon, fame, money, personal relationships, popularity, health ... The wise person sees the advantages of all of these but also knows that they may – before too long, at a time of fate's choosing – have to draw the borders right back and find contentment within a more bounded space.

*

The wise emerge as realistic about the consequences of winning and succeeding. They may want to win as much as the next person, but they are aware of how many fundamentals will remain unchanged, whatever the outcome. They don't exaggerate the transformations available to us. They know how much we remain tethered to some basic dynamics in our personalities, whatever job we have or material possession we acquire. This is both cautionary (for those who succeed) and hopeful (for those who won't). The wise see the continuities across those two categories over-emphasised by modern consumer capitalism: 'success' and 'failure'.

*

In our ambitious age, it is common to begin with dreams of being able to pull off an unblemished life, where one can hope to get the major decisions – in love and work – right. But the wise realise that it is impossible to fashion a spotless life; one will make some extremely large and utterly uncorrectable errors in a number of areas. Perfectionism is a wicked illusion. Regret is unavoidable. But regret lessens the more we see that error is endemic across the species. One can't look at anyone's life story without seeing some devastating mistakes etched across it. These errors are not coincidental but structural; they arise because we all lack the information we need to make choices in time-sensitive situations. We are all, where it counts, steering almost blind.

*

The wise know that turmoil is always around the corner – and they have come to fear and sense its approach. That's why they nurture such a strong commitment to calm. A quiet evening feels like an achievement. A day without anxiety is something to be celebrated. They are not afraid of having a somewhat boring time. There could, and will again, be so much worse.

*

Precisely because some relationships have had a great, intimate, loving purpose, they can get completed. A relationship can be finished in the way that childhood can be finished: a child – thanks to the immense devotion of their parents – arrives at a point at which, in order to progress further, they need to leave home. They're not being kicked out in anger or running away in despair; they're leaving because the work of childhood has been done. It isn't a rejection of love; it is love's good consequence. Two people ending a relationship doesn't have to be a sign of their failure; it can be the sign that they have taught one another everything they know – and helped one another as much as they can.

*

A strong desire not to be alone is generally a sure sign that one is incubating, and warding off, an important yet painful realisation.

*

# 3. Sociability

Great conversations are as rare as a beautiful square in a foreign city that one stumbles on at night and then doesn't know how to get back to in the daytime.

\*

Friends are less critical of us than our partners, not because they're any kinder or understand things more clearly; they just care a lot less.

\*

Most people could be bearable if they could only acknowledge how peculiar they are. It's the insistence on normality that kills the spirit.

\*

As successful self-propagandists know, the main source of information for how things are going with us is us.

\*

Being on the receiving end of hypocritical politeness may feel grating – but at least people are bothering to lie.

\*

A 'good reputation' wouldn't matter quite so much if people were more in the habit of judging others on their own merits.

*

There are people we would long ago have forgotten all about if they hadn't started to ignore us.

*

Seeing through people is so easy – and it gets you no-where.

*

We mostly lose our tempers, not with those who are actually to blame but with those who love us enough to forgive us our foul moods.

*

It can be awkward to say to a friend, 'I need cheering up for the misery your success has caused me.'

*

Definition of an egoist: someone insufficiently interested in me.

\*

For paranoia about 'what other people think': remember that only some hate, a very few love – and almost all just don't care.

\*

Acquiring enemies may feel like a sign that one's life has gone wrong, but it's more likely to be an indication that one has found a few things to believe in.

\*

Getting to the top always has an unfortunate tendency to persuade people that the system is OK after all.

\*

So many of life's problems would be softened if we had three or four exceptional friends living within a two-minute radius.

\*

Most anger stems from a desperate sense of weakness and fear – hard to remember when one is at the receiving end of its defiant roar.

∗

Equation of fame: to be quite liked by two people requires you to be known to a thousand, to be actively hated by twenty and to mildly irritate a hundred.

∗

People who need to be alone a lot, who are asphyxiated without periods by themselves, take others a lot more seriously than the uncomplicatedly gregarious. They are aware of how much effort it really takes to be present with another human – and how joyful, but also exhausting and frightening it may be too. The properly sociable don't have the strength to spend very much time in others' company.

∗

We end up lonely because it seems so implausible to us that other people might be lonely too.

∗

We may be drawn to solitude, not because we despise humanity but because we are properly responsive to what the company of others entails. Extensive stretches of being alone may, in reality, be a precondition for knowing how to be a better friend and a properly attentive companion.

*

It is hard to deepen a friendship with anyone who hasn't had close-up experience of profound despair.

*

Definition of a present: something you can't get for yourself. As a child, that meant toys. In adulthood: reassurance, sympathy, forgiveness.

*

One of the fundamental paths to sympathy is the power to hold on, in the most challenging situations, to a distinction between a person's overt unpleasant actions and the more poignant motives that may underlie them. Pure evil is seldom at work. Almost all our worst moments can be traced back to an unexotic, bathetic, temptingly neglected ingredient: pain.

*

It is sad enough when two people dislike each other. It is even sadder when two people fail to connect because both parties defensively but falsely guess that the other doesn't like them – and yet, out of low self-worth, don't take any risk whatsoever to alter the situation. We should stop worrying quite so much whether or not people like us and make that far more interesting and socially useful move: concentrate on showing that we like them.

\*

A helpful way to kickstart conversation at dinner: 'So what was everyone frightened of today?'

\*

Bookshops are a valuable destination for the lonely, given all the books that have been written because authors couldn't find anyone to talk to.

\*

Love means making the effort to extend our compassion beyond the bounds of attraction so that we may look generously on all those we might at first glance have deemed beyond the pale or 'undeserving'.

\*

It is love when we can look at someone who appears misguided, lazy, entitled, angry or proud and, instead of labelling them despicable, are able to wonder with imagination and sympathy how they might have come to be this way, when we can perceive the lost, vulnerable or hurt youngster that must lie somewhere within the perplexing or dispiriting adult.

*

All nastiness is, at heart, a symptom of pain and unfulfillment. We can't know exactly what the other's problem is, but we can be assured that there is one. And while we may not be able to get back directly at our enemies, by a strange piece of cosmic justice, we can know that something or someone has got there first, for their behaviour is all the proof we should need of the scale of their pre-existing misery.

*

The pity-filled person recognises how desperate our condition is, but what subverts their efforts to be properly kind is the energy with which they make it clear that our sorrow is ours and ours alone – and that they will not, and could never, be touched by any similar horror. They want to be sweet to us, of course, but what they will not do is recognise that they are as open to foolishness, accident and suffering as we are. They need – from fear – to create a solid wall between our condition and theirs. They need to remind us, and most importantly themselves, that they are firmly rooted on dry land, while we are out there drowning in the ocean swell. They will throw us a small life raft perhaps; what they don't want to imagine is ever needing one themselves.

*

Being snappy is a symptom of a frank discussion we forgot to have some way back.

*

However convenient it would be if people could be born friendly and empathise spontaneously with the pains of others, the human mind seems too sluggish and selfish an instrument to properly imagine what suffering might look like for someone else until it has been energetically goaded on by its own agonies. Empathy can solely be forged by personal suffering. To be a good friend, one has no option other than to have had close-up, personal experience of terrible times.

*

Once we have a clearer sense of what we're looking for in social life, we can, with relief, politely back out from so many of our less fruitful acquaintanceships – and concentrate our affection and interest on the very small number of people who properly honour the core functions of friendship. We should feel extremely lucky if we manage to lay claim to three friends worthy of the title in a lifetime.

*

It is very normal, and highly understandable, for properly social people – that is, people who really wish their souls to connect with those of others – to feel anxious about parties – and to prefer to see people very seldom and then only in the smallest and most intimate of contexts. If we properly crave the love and understanding of people, it will be too much to bear the humiliations and betrayals involved in the average get-together. We should restrict our social lives to the exceptional evening out with a true friend who can weep with us, sympathise with us and exchange authentic and heartfelt notes with us on the fleeting ecstasies and long-running challenges of being human. That will be a 'party' worth breaking our isolation for.

\*

The more we need other people to know something, the less we may be able to secure the serene frame of mind, which is indispensable if we are to convey it to them effectively.

\*

Even if we haven't signed up to instruct adolescents in maths or languages, even if we aren't interested in telling someone how to find the area of a circle or ask for a train ticket in French, we are called upon to 'teach' almost every hour of every day. We have to teach others how we're feeling, what we want, what is paining us. In other words, the teaching specialisation we have to take on throughout our lives comprises a bizarre sounding but crucial and enormous subject: Who I Am, How I Feel and What I Care About. We've fatally misconstrued teaching as a specific professional job, when it's in actuality a basic psychological manoeuvre upon which the health of every community, family, relationship and office depends.

\*

We may need occasionally to despair of someone – as the price to pay for keeping faith with ourselves.

\*

The single greatest spur towards a loving perspective on others is a live awareness that we are also deeply imperfect. The enemy of generosity is the sense that we might be beyond fault – whereas love begins when we can acknowledge that we are in equal measures idiotic, mentally wobbly and flawed. It's an implicit faith in their own perfection that turns people into unbearably harsh judges.

*

Looking at the world through the eyes of love, we are forced to conclude that there is no such thing as a simply bad person and no such thing as a monster. There is only ever pain, anxiety and suffering that have coalesced into unfortunate action. This isn't just a kind thought; it happens – more usefully – to be the truth.

*

The best judge of someone's intent towards us can be discerned by how they leave us feeling about ourselves rather than what they overtly talk about.

*

We can get a good sense of what certain people worry about by paying careful attention to what we find ourselves worrying about in their company.

*

Whatever the impression we might have that everyone is furious all the time, the larger problem is people's widespread inability to get angry, their failure to know how rightly and effectively to mount a complaint, their inarticulate swallowing of frustration – and the bitterness, subterranean 'acting out' and low-level depression that follow. For every one person who shouts too loudly, there are at least twenty who have unfairly lost their voices.

*

The true answer to snobbery is not to deny that there is such a thing as a better or a worse person; it's to insist that we are such poor judges of the worth of others, we're unlikely to be able to discern the difference – and so our prevailing duty is to remain kind, good, curious and imaginative about pretty much everyone who crosses our path.

*

We are liable to have spent a large chunk of our lives in an essentially passive relationship to everyday infringements by people close to us. But we aren't a piece of helpless flotsam on the river of others' wishes; we have agency, direction and – as it were – a rudder. The price we need to pay for affection isn't compliance. We can gradually take on board a highly implausible-sounding yet redemptive notion: that we can prove loveable and worthy of respect and at the same time, when the occasion demands it, as it probably will a few times every day, utter a warm-sounding but definitive 'no'.

*

We become properly invested in being kind when we realise the power we possess in most situations to condemn another human to a few hours of self-hatred – or, by a few well-aimed remarks, to remind them of their value and contribution to existence.

*

We can't go wrong being around people: either they will be kind, and we will derive reassurance and support, or they will be hurtful and annoying, and we will thereby acquire a raft of new ideas for our ongoing research into that perennially fascinating topic: The Awfulness of Others.

*

The tragedy of modern technology is that it has enabled us to know far too much about the contents of others' minds – and thereby rendered a high and vigilant degree of misanthropy inevitable.

*

Civilisation and trust in human nature ended in the early summer of 2007 – the last summer before that new kind of phone.

*

A failure: someone who desperately needs others to fail.

*

Much of modern society amounts to a concerted conspiracy to prevent people from thinking freely, peacefully and imaginatively on their own.

*

If someone can neither teach us something new nor reassure us in our fears, we should stay home.

*

Anyone who fails to find themselves ridiculous will, over time, be insufferable.

*

A 'nice person' just means someone who doesn't generally assume they are very nice.

*

Given how important being successful is said to be, it's notable that, almost always, the nicest (and funniest) people to be around are those convinced, often to the point of wanting to end matters, that they have made a mess of their lives.

*

Wanting to impress strangers and wanting to have friends: the two ambitions should be recognised as plainly incompatible.

*

What separates bitter from merely sad people are the former's background belief that life should have been fair. They are unappealing chiefly through their tetchy failure to grasp the tragic nature of the human condition.

*

We are constantly undermining our vows, taken in the wake of another encounter, never to see certain people ever again. We forgive too easily. We rarely have the ruthlessness of our gut instincts.

*

The kindest, most pleasant people are those who easily, and without pride, quickly imagine they might be in the wrong.

*

It takes an uncommon degree of maturity and self-acceptance to overcome the impulse to take joy in the failure of others.

*

We should at once be suspicious of anyone who claims to 'love people'. As a group, in totality, the species should – of course – be experienced only as profoundly troubling.

*

People who really understand friendship have few friends – even, dare one say it, no friends.

*

Other people are always far more likely to be as we know we are – with all our quirks, fragilities, compulsions and surprising aspects – than they are to be like the apparently 'normal' people they suggest they are.

*

A truth as basic as it is inviolable: other people are nasty because they are in pain. The only reason they hurt us is because they are – somewhere deep inside – hurting themselves. No one solid ever consciously strips another of their happiness.

*

Cynics are – beneath it all – only idealists with awkwardly high standards.

*

Love is the effort required to imagine oneself more accurately into the life of another human who has not made it in any way easy to admire or even like them.

*

The best cure for one's bad tendencies is to observe them fully developed in someone else.

*

Anyone who isn't embarrassed of who they were last year probably isn't learning enough.

*

People only start to get interesting when they start to rattle the bars of their cages.

*

Everyone's life is messed up. All that varies is how obvious this is to others.

*

Almost everyone is worried rather than mean.

*

Most people are more deserving of pity than censure.

*

At its core, the idea of charity goes far beyond giving money. It is about interpreting others' lives with imagination. It involves perceiving that their difficult behaviour is not a sign of wickedness or sin, but of suffering.

*

The clarity of midnight: the capacity to think well is inversely related to the number of people in the area who are awake.

*

In theory, we all love kindness, of course, but in practice, a kind person sounds like something we would try to be only once every other more arduous and more rewarding alternative had failed. Learning to be kind means acknowledging, and overcoming the sense of, how boring kindness can sound.

*

What we tend to be most short of from others is kindness of interpretation, that is, a generous perspective on the weaknesses, eccentricities, anxieties and follies that we present but are unable to win direct sympathy for. The kind person retells the story of our lives in a redemptive way.

*

The kind person works with a picture of us that is sufficiently generous and complex as to make us more than just the 'fool' or 'weirdo', the 'failure' or 'loser' that we might otherwise so easily have been dismissed as.

*

The kind person gives generously from a sense that they too will stand in need of kindness. Not right now, not over this, but in some other area. They know that self-righteousness is merely the result of a faulty memory, an inability to hold in mind – at moments when they are truly good and totally in the right – how often they have been deeply and definitively in the wrong.

*

We should always strive to see people's weaknesses as the inevitable downside of certain merits that drew us to them, and from which we will benefit at other points (even if none of these benefits are apparent right now). What we're seeing are not their faults, pure and simple, but rather the shadow side of things that are genuinely good about them. We're picking up on weaknesses that derive from strengths.

*

Kindness remembers how there might still be virtue amidst a lot of evil. Kindness is aware that when someone shouts an insult, they are not usually revealing the secret truth about their feelings; they are trying to wound the other because they feel they have been hurt – usually by someone else, whom they don't have the authority to injure back. Kindness is interested in mitigating circumstances, in bits of the truth that can cast a less catastrophic light on folly.

\*

Kind people have overcome the unhelpful idea that – if one looks harder – it would be possible to find someone who was always perfect to be around. If strengths are invariably connected to failings, there won't be anyone who is remotely flawless. We may well find people with different strengths, but they will also have a new litany of weaknesses. It's always necessary to take a moment to remind ourselves that perfect people don't exist.

\*

The modern world is currently very uncomfortable around the idea of a good person not succeeding. We'd rather say that they weren't good at all than embrace a far more disturbing and less well-publicised thought: that – in fact – the world is very unfair. Kind people keep the notion of injustice always in mind.

\*

One of the most fundamental paths to remaining kind around people is the power to hold on, even in very challenging situations, to a distinction between what someone does – and what they meant to do.

\*

When we carry an excess of self-disgust around with us, operating just below the radar of conscious awareness, we'll constantly seek confirmation from the wider world that we really are the worthless people we take ourselves to be. It's natural to see meanness everywhere when we see ourselves as fitting targets for insult.

\*

We're seldom very good at perceiving what motives happen to be involved in the incidents that hurt us. We are easily and wildly mistaken. We see intention where there was none and escalate and confront when no strenuous or agitated responses are warranted.

*

Part of the reason why we jump so readily to dark conclusions about other people and see plots to insult and harm us is a rather poignant psychological phenomenon: self-hatred. The less we like ourselves, the more we appear in our own eyes as really rather plausible targets for mockery and harm. That is why being kind must involve first learning to be kind to oneself.

*

The greatest kindness we can bestow on others in difficult moments is to treat them as if they were children. We rarely feel personally agitated or wounded by the bad behaviour of small children. And the reason is that we don't assign negative motives or mean intentions to them. We reach around for the most benevolent interpretations. We forgive.

*

It's very touching that we live in a world where we have learnt to be so kind to children; it would be even kinder if we learnt to be a little more generous towards the child-like parts of one another.

*

'Never say that people are evil,' wrote the French philosopher Émile-Auguste Chartier. 'You just need to look for the pin.' What he meant was, don't merely condemn; look for the source of the jabbing pain that drives a person to behave in certain irritating or appalling ways.

*

We need always to imagine the turmoil, disappointment, worry and sadness in people who may outwardly appear merely aggressive and 'bad'. We need to aim compassion in an unexpected place: at those who annoy us most.

*

Kind people know all about filtering their thoughts. They understand that being 'themselves' is a treat they must take enormous pains to spare everyone else from experiencing – especially anyone they claim to care about.

*

The politely kind person is so aware of their own dislikable sides, they nimbly minimise their impact upon the world. It is their suspicion of themselves that helps them be – in everyday life – uncommonly friendly, trustworthy and nice.

*

The kind person works with an underlying sense that other people are internally very fragile. Those around them are felt – without insult – to be forever on the verge of self-hatred. Their egos are assumed to be gossamer thin and at perpetual risk of deflating. Kind people, therefore, let out constant small signals of reassurance and affirmation.

*

Kind people know that however confident we may look, we are painfully vulnerable to a sense of being disliked and taken for granted. All of us are walking around without a skin. Therefore, scattering flattering remarks isn't devious or slick; it helps everyone to endure themselves.

*

All of us get a bit unbalanced in one way or another: too serious, too gloomy, too jokey. And so we all benefit from being tugged back towards a healthier mean. The good teaser latches onto and responds to our distinctive imbalances and gets compassionately constructive about trying to change us, not by delivering a stern lesson but by helping us to notice our excesses and laugh at them. We sense the teaser trying to give us a useful little shove in a good (and secretly welcome) direction and therefore know that, at its affectionate best, teasing is at once sweet and constructive.

*

Perhaps the most instructive question we can ask of a good friend – the question that teaches us most about where we might have lost perspective – is simply, what do I need to be teased about?

*

Kind people accept that they may never be able to transform another person's prospects entirely, but their modesty around what is possible makes them acutely sensitive to the worth of the little things: they are always ready for a smile, they remember birthdays, they write postcards and devote time to friendly chats.

*

Kind people work with a conception of the world in which good and bad are deviously entangled and in which bits of the truth are always showing up in unfamiliar guises in unexpected people. They don't judge quickly. Their careful politeness is a logical response to the complexity they identify in themselves and in the world.

*

Kind people know how to make confessions. They give those they talk to access to a very necessary and consoling sense of their own errors, humiliations and follies – insights with which others can begin to judge themselves and their sad and compulsive sides more compassionately.

*

What enables the kind person to please is their capacity to hold on in social encounters, even with rather intimidating and alien-seeming people, to an intimate knowledge of what satisfies, consoles and cheers them. They instinctively use their own experience as a base for thinking about the needs of others.

\*

Kind people know how to be a little shy. Shyness has its insightful dimensions. It is infused with an awareness that we might be bothering someone with our presence; it is based upon an acute sense that a stranger could be dissatisfied or discomfited by us. The shy person is touchingly alive to the dangers of being a nuisance.

\*

Kind people know that however solid and dignified someone appears on the outside, behind the scenes there will inevitably be a struggling self, potentially awkward, easily bemused, beset by physical appetites, on the verge of loneliness – and frequently in need of nothing more subtle or elevated than a hug or a cheering chat.

\*

Kind people know that great truths ('I really like you') sometimes have to pass into the mind of another person via a smaller falsehood ('I loved your cake/party/book').

*

However much they love the truth, kind people have an even greater commitment to something else: being nice. They grasp (and make allowances for) the ease with which a truth can produce desperately unhelpful convictions in the minds of others and are therefore not proudly over-committed to complete honesty at every turn. Their loyalty is reserved for something they take to be far more important than literal narration: the well-being of their audiences.

*

Kind people reveal plenty about their own failings. They confess not so much to unburden themselves as to help others accept their own nature and see that sometimes being a bad parent, a poor lover or a confused worker are not malignant acts of wickedness but ordinary features of being alive that others have unfairly edited out of their public profiles.

*

Kind people know that the existence of highly trouble-some elements in others doesn't preclude the simulta-neous presence of vast zones of goodness, humility and benevolence. They know that everyone's right to charity, attention and friendship should not be irrevocably lost on the basis of some darker sides. While hoping it might be otherwise, kind people simply take it for granted that decent humans constantly do and think not very nice things.

*

Kind people are interesting not because they have done extraordinary things, but because they are attentive, self-aware listeners and reliable, honest correspond-ents of the tremors of their own minds and hearts. They thereby give us faithful and fascinating accounts of the pathos, drama and strangeness of being alive.

*

At the right points, interesting people know how to be themselves. It feels significant that most five-year-olds are far less boring than most forty-five-year-olds. What makes these children gripping is not so much that they have more interesting feelings than anyone else (far from it), but that they are especially uncensored correspondents of these feelings. Their inexperience of the world means they are still instinctively loyal to themselves – as kind, charming adults remember to be.

\*

The person we call interesting is, in essence, someone alive to what we all deeply want from social intercourse: an uncensored glimpse of what the brief waking dream called life looks like through the eyes of another person and the reassurance that we are not entirely alone with all that feels most bewildering, peculiar and intense within us.

\*

It's deeply poignant that we should expend so much effort on trying to look strong before the world – when, all the while, it's really only ever the revelation of the somewhat embarrassing, sad, melancholy and anxious bits of us that makes us endearing to others and transforms strangers into friends.

*

We should stop expecting people to be anything other than very flawed. Whomever we got to know would be radically imperfect in a host of deeply serious ways. There can only ever be 'good enough' relationships with others.

*

We shouldn't blame other people for failing to know us as we want to be known. They are not tragically inept. No one properly and entirely understands, and can therefore fully sympathise with, anyone else.

*

If we are not regularly and very deeply embarrassed about who we are, it can only be because we haven't begun to understand ourselves.

*

Kindness is founded on an active sense of how difficult one is to be around. We should be gentle with anyone who has agreed to take on the arduous task of spending their days and nights with us.

*

We should accept that, in many situations, other people will be wiser, more reasonable and more mature than we are. We should want to learn from them. We should bear having things pointed out to us. We should, at key points, see them as the teachers and ourselves as pupils.

*

How badly we react to frustration is critically determined by what we think of as normal. We aren't overwhelmed by anger whenever something goes wrong. Our greatest furies spring from events that violate our sense of the ground rules of existence. A degree of pessimism is the royal route to patience.

*

People in general range from the merely imperfect to the truly awful. At best, we can move from seeing others as idiots to viewing them as that far more tolerable and truly kind alternative: loveable idiots.

*

# 4. **Work**

An average life might be only 600,000 hours long; we could sometimes do with frightening ourselves a little into making a change.

\*

We may seek a fortune for no greater reason than to secure the respect and attention of people who would otherwise look straight through us.

\*

People who feel powerful rarely have a strong need to become so.

\*

Decadence involves a forgetting of how privilege is gained, which brings about its loss.

\*

To judge by the amount of productive thinking that goes on there, most beds have a better claim to be called offices than offices.

\*

Some careers prove to be too short to allow latent talent to flourish; others are too long not to let latent idiocy play itself out.

*

The logic to not leaving enough time to get to a frightening meeting: the fear of being late displaces the fear of the encounter.

*

Companies are often like confused teenagers: requiring dauntingly long to work out 'who they really are'.

*

One millimetre outside their area of expertise, geniuses can be counted on to be as silly as the rest of us.

*

Work is most fulfilling when we are at the comfortable, exciting edge of not quite knowing what we are doing.

*

Wealth is not an absolute. It is relative to desire. Every time we yearn for something we cannot afford, we grow poorer, whatever our resources. And every time we feel satisfied with what we have, we can be counted as rich, however little we may actually possess.

*

What ends up aging and eventually killing us isn't one big thing but thousands of tiny obligations, which we don't have the heart to push away, which all seem relatively minor, but which collectively have the power to finish us off.

*

One of the finest protections against disappointment is to have a lot going on.

*

To a humiliating (but helpful) extent, some of the gravest problems we face during a day can be traced back to a brutally simple fact: we have not had enough sleep.

*

To have a chance to achieve something that will one day be in the news, we have to spend quite a lot of time away from the news.

\*

A so-called 'meaningful' job is any occupation that leaves us feeling, at the close of the day, that we have somehow either decreased the suffering or increased the satisfaction of another human being.

\*

Power is the displacement activity for those who are barred, on the grounds of increasing age or of marriage vows, from the pursuit of love.

\*

Reputation is a bit like a table: one or two marks and everyone notices; a whole host of scratches and things start to blend in.

\*

Office life would not be possible without the hard take-offs and landings effected by coffee and alcohol.

\*

It is humbling that most of our best thoughts come to us precisely – and only – when we have made no conscious attempt to think.

\*

People who don't believe in us: those unwitting, continuous sources of motivation.

\*

Sunday angst is trying in its own confused way to tell us something worth listening to: we must change our lives.

\*

Profit is the reward for correctly understanding an aspect of reality ahead of our peers.

\*

Most business meetings involve one party elaborately suppressing a wish to shout at the other, 'Give us the money.'

\*

We should never check a phone if we don't have the time or energy to deal with the bad news it might contain.

*

We accuse children of silliness for fighting over small things only because they lack access to the big things that we deem it acceptable to fight over.

*

We shouldn't feel embarrassed by our failures, only by an inability to grow anything useful or instructive from them.

*

A key moment in history: the first person who felt they had 'too much going on'.

*

Our minds wait until we are not asking anything of them to yield their best material.

*

We shouldn't feign surprise that celebrities might be 'thin skinned'. Who else would work so hard for reputation other than those who cared a bit too much what others thought?

*

The more we like what we've written, the less we need others to approve.

*

The fear of saying something stupid (which stupid people never have) has censored far more good ideas than bad ones.

*

We're taught so much about how to succeed. There is almost nothing to help us cope with the statistically far more likely possibility that we will fail.

*

A society that thinks of itself as meritocratic converts poverty from a condition of honourable, if painful, bad luck into evidence of personal incompetence. It increases the burden of failure exponentially.

*

There is no family in the land without a serious disaster in their midst. Look at a classroom of twenty sweet five-year-olds – within half a century, a good third of them will have been scarred by a very sharp knife indeed. We could tell the story of humanity not – as we usually do – as one of progress and gradual mastery, but as one of repeated distress, unshakeable madness and eternal regret. Almost no life goes to plan; few of us come through unscathed, and it's questionable whether all our beautiful machines and complicated accomplishments have made us one jot less troubled than our animal-skin-clad foraging ancestors.

*

It would rarely occur to anyone who did not harbour a high degree of self-suspicion to undertake so many outsized efforts to impress and to make a mark upon the world.

*

Perfectionism does not spring from a love of perfection. It has its origins in a feeling of never being good enough. It is rooted in self-hatred – sparked by memories of being disapproved of or neglected by those who should more fairly have esteemed us warmly in childhood. We become perfectionists from a primary sense of being unworthy. We aren't interested in perfect work at all; we are trying to escape from a feeling of being awful people. Manic work is just the medium through which we are striving to grow tolerable in our own eyes.

*

People don't kill themselves because bad things happen to them; they kill themselves because they are already suffering from intense self-hatred, which an unfortunate event or two serves to corroborate and then expand into an unanswerable argument for ending things.

*

The most obvious, rarely mentioned prediction about the future is that it will share most of its characteristics with the past.

*

Most of what goes wrong in our lives is not, in the end, the result of a failure of raw effort or busyness. We come to grief, not because we haven't rushed around enough or put in a sufficient number of hours; we do so because there has, somewhere along the way, been a shortfall in thinking. We have not allowed ourselves a requisite number of hours in which we looked as if we were doing 'nothing': gazing out of the window, following a trail of clouds across the evening sky, lying in a bath, walking around a park or writing down a few notes in a journal, in other words, apparently empty hours of reflection when life's real work unfolds – our worst mistakes can be caught and our best opportunities identified.

*

Our preoccupation with money has a poignant and un-expected cause: we keep wanting more money than we need because we haven't as yet identified a passion that could render us indifferent to modest clothes and circumstances. We haven't yet discovered what we love.

*

What helps enormously in our attempts to know our own minds is, surprisingly, the presence of another mind. For all the glamour of the solitary seer, thinking can sometimes happen best in tandem. It is the curiosity of someone else that gives us the confidence to remain curious about ourselves. It is the application of a light pressure from outside us that firms up the jumbled impressions within. The requirement to verbalise our confusions mobilises our flabby reserves of concentration.

*

Tragedy teaches us that the most shocking events can befall the more or less innocent or the only averagely muddled and weak. We do not inhabit a properly moral universe, disaster is at points distributed to those who could not have expected it to be a fair outcome, given what they did. A loving perspective accepts a remarkable, frightening and still-too-seldom accepted possibility: that bad things befall good people.

*

Effective thinking isn't – unfortunately – about 'working hard' in any brute or rote sense; it is about learning to spot, defend, nurture and grow our fleeting, tentative periods of insight.

＊

There are few catastrophes, in our own lives or in those of nations, that do not ultimately have their origins in a shortfall of emotional intelligence.

＊

We should observe how often and how naturally we devote our time to executing our ideas before we have submitted them to adequate scrutiny; we should note our discomfort around questions like, why is this a worthwhile effort? Where will I really be in a few years if this goes right? How is this connected up with what fulfills me? What is the point here? And we should watch our comparative enthusiasm for launching ourselves into projects in a hurry, for fretting only about the lower-level procedural hiccups and for ensuring that we are too 'busy' ever to leave time for reflection. We should grow suspicious of our covert preference for franticness over enquiry.

＊

The more interesting or pertinent our thoughts happen to be, the more they have a tendency to escape our grasp. It seems as though there is a devilish correlation between how important and necessary a thought is to us and how likely it is to elude our command. The truly precious thoughts have something almost airborne about them, so inclined are they to flit away from us at the slightest approach of our conscious selves.

*

A shower emerges as one of the best places on earth in which to do any serious reflection. Amidst the crashing water and the steam and with a few minutes of respite before the day starts, the mind is no longer on guard. We're not meant to be thinking and so – at last – we can think freely and courageously.

*

Our world places a very high premium on good ideas – but spends very little serious effort in investigating why we find it extraordinarily hard to hatch them. We should learn that the real enemy of good thinking isn't a small desk or a modest view; it is – almost always – anxiety.

*

Not all good ideas have yet been had – and our minds are as good a place as any in which they might one day hatch.

\*

Outwardly idling does not have to mean that we are neglecting to be fruitful. It may look to the world as if we are accomplishing nothing at all but, below the surface, a lot may be going on that's both important and, in its own way, very arduous. When we're busy with routines and administration, we're focused on the elements that sit at the front of our minds; we're executing plans rather than reflecting on their value and ultimate purpose. But it is to the deeper, less accessible zones of our inner lives that we have to turn in order to understand the foundations of our problems and arrive at decisions and conclusions that can govern our overall path. Yet these only emerge – shyly and tentatively – when we are feeling brave enough to distance ourselves from immediate demands, when we can stare at clouds and do so-called nothing at all.

\*

We have read more than Socrates; we have had as many
– if not more – experiences than Plato.

\*

We need to distinguish between emotional and practical
hard work. Someone who looks extremely active, whose
diary is filled from morning till night, who is always running to answer messages and meet clients may appear
the opposite of lazy. But secretly, there may be a lot of
avoidance going on beneath the outward frenzy. Busy
people evade a different order of undertaking. They are
practically a hive of activity, yet they don't get round to
working out their real feelings about their work. They
constantly delay the investigation of their own direction. They are lazy when it comes to understanding particular emotions about a partner or friend. They go to
every conference but don't get around to thinking what
their status means to them; they catch up regularly with
colleagues but don't consider what the point of money
might be. Their busyness is a subtle but powerful form
of distraction.

\*

The best way to separate out ambition from fear is to ask oneself what one would do if one could not fail.

\*

Our minds are, in general, a great deal readier to execute than to reflect. They can be rendered deeply uncomfortable by so-called large questions: what am I really trying to do? What do I actually enjoy and who am I trying to please? How would I feel if what I'm currently doing comes right? What will I regret in a decade's time? By contrast, the easy bit can be the running around, the never pausing to ask why, the repeatedly ensuring that there isn't a moment to have doubts or feel sad or be searching. Busyness can mask a vicious form of laziness.

\*

An average office is filled with so much psychoanalytic complexity that the idea of being able to be 'professional' (and for others to be so back) is a prelude to constant puzzlement and disappointment. It would be gentler on our nerves to accept from the first that we are operating in an asylum that has no wish to recognise itself as such.

\*

When we come to know the true price some ways of life exact, we may slowly realise we are not willing to pay for the envy, fear, deceit and anxiety. Our days are limited on the earth. We may – for the sake of true riches – willingly, and with no loss of dignity, opt to become a little more reclusive, temperate and obscure.

*

Those who put up the skyscrapers, write the bestselling books, perform on stage or make partner may, in fact, be the unwell ones. Whereas the characters who – without agony – can bear an ordinary life, the so-called contented 'mediocrities', may in fact be the emotional superstars, the aristocrats of the spirit, the captains of the heart. The world divides into the privileged who can be ordinary and the damned who are compelled to be remarkable.

*

We spend the greater part of a lifetime trying to impress people who will be happy when we're dead.

*

One of the less well observed preconditions for being able to find a good job is self-love, a background (often elusive) sense that we deserve to be professionally fulfilled.

\*

Rather than reject glamour, the priority is to redirect it more accurately. In the utopia, the following things would be glamorous: forgiveness, depressive realism, the acceptance of imperfection, humility, gratitude ... In other words, glamour would support, rather than undermine, the pursuit of a wise life.

\*

No one would want to be famous who hadn't also, somewhere in the past, been made to feel extremely insignificant.

\*

Procrastination is often mistaken for laziness, but really it is – always – a species of terror at the possible consequences of messing up.

*

We overcome procrastination, not by berating ourselves to 'work harder' but by attempting to weaken the background punishing perfectionism that is responsible for stalling us with fear.

*

We all have very similar and very able minds; where geniuses differ is in their more robust inclinations to study them properly and hold on more bravely to their contents.

*

One wants to be famous out of a desire for kindness. But the world isn't generally kind to the famous for very long. The reason is basic: the success of any one person involves humiliation for lots of others. The celebrity of a few people will always contrast painfully with the obscurity of the many. Being famous upsets people.

*

Fame really just means you get noticed a great deal – not that you get understood, appreciated or loved.

*

The sign of good parenting: when a child has no wish to become famous.

*

For most of history, the majority of humans have believed that this life is not the only chance we get to fulfill ourselves. There will be other lives beyond death, in which we will be able to correct the errors made here on earth. Career anxiety stems – in part – from a growing inability to believe in after lives.

*

We pin our hopes for happiness on love and work. And yet, in relation to both, refuse to plan methodically, to understand ourselves thoroughly, to train relentlessly and to go into therapy before we act. We worship instinct in precisely the wrong places.

*

The witching hour for career crises is late Sunday afternoon, usually 5 p.m., when the vague hopes and sense of possibility of the weekend finally crash into the cold realities of the week ahead. The extent of our despair is a measure of our degree of untapped potential.

∗

Career anxiety is our latent talent howling through our minds, desperate not to go to the grave unspent.

∗

The modern meaning of life: that our deepest interests should find external expression in a form that others will find useful – and that will bring in sufficient money to fund a bourgeois life. We deserve pity for the scale of what we now consider normal.

∗

It is only in very recent history that we have even attempted not just to make money at work, but also – extraordinarily – to be happy there as well. How deeply peculiar the idea would have sounded to most of our ancestors, especially the aristocrats who never worked and the working classes who mostly would strongly have wanted not to. Happy work is the genius, malevolent invention of the bourgeoisie.

\*

We reassure ourselves about the amount time we have left by pegging our imagined death to the date of the average lifespan, without remembering that long before we reach that terminal point, we will have passed through years of growing infirmity, terror as our friends die off, a sense that we no longer feel at home in the world and humiliating bladder problems. In other words, we must never hold back from a useful panic at how little time there is left.

\*

Given how consequential the issue it treats is, how extraordinary it is that career counselling should still be the most amateur of occupations – about as haphazard as medieval brain surgery.

\*

Many of us are still trapped within the career cage unwittingly created for us by some hasty choices made by our unknowing eighteen-year-old selves.

\*

When a job feels meaningful, we would be ready to lay our lives down for it and ask only for a salary roughly equivalent to the minimum wage. When we know it ultimately makes no sense, we quibble over millions. Soldiers and nurses vs bankers.

\*

Our prospective working lives are like Russian dolls. There are at least five utterly plausible career selves within each of us. We are multiple beings in a vain search for singular identities.

\*

Every moment of frustration signals a potential new business waiting to be born.

＊

People who are able to get anything done are those able to forgive themselves the horror of the first draft.

＊

The people who most care about us never especially admire our achievements; they liked us all along anyway.

＊

When we feel self-important and essential to a task, we should remember General de Gaulle's maxim: 'The cemeteries of France are full of "indispensible" men.'

＊

Those who are envied are themselves painfully envious of others.

＊

Work begins when the fear of doing something badly is finally outstripped by the fear of doing nothing at all.

＊

However mediocre we may feel, there is already immense skill, joy and nobility involved in bringing up a child to be reasonably independent and balanced, in maintaining a wobbly but decent relationship with a partner over many years despite areas of extreme difficulty, in keeping a home in reasonable order, in getting a lot of early nights, in doing a not very exciting or well-paid job responsibly and cheerfully, in listening properly to other people and, in general, in not succumbing to madness or rage at the paradox and compromises involved in being alive. We are doing well enough already.

\*

At the heart of a lot of under-confidence is a skewed picture of how normal a dignified life might be. We imagine it might be possible to place ourselves beyond mockery. We trust that it is an option to lead a good life without regularly making complete idiots of ourselves.

\*

The way to greater confidence isn't to reassure ourselves of our own dignity; it's to grow at peace with the inevitable nature of our ridiculousness. We are idiots now, we have been idiots in the past, and we will be idiots again in the future. There aren't any other available options for human beings.

*

We grow timid when we allow ourselves to be taken in by the respectable sides of others. Such are the pains people take to appear sane, we collectively create a phantasm – problematic for everyone – which suggests that normality might be possible for many. In reality, no one is normal.

*

Once we learn to see ourselves as already, and by nature, foolish, it really doesn't matter so much if we do one more thing that might look quite stupid. Failure won't be news to us; it will only confirm what we have already gracefully accepted in our hearts long ago: that we, like every other person on the earth, are limitless buffoons.

*

The road to greater confidence begins with a ritual of telling oneself solemnly every morning, before heading out for the day, that one is a muttonhead, a cretin, a dumbbell and an imbecile. One or two more acts of folly should, thereafter, not matter very much at all.

*

The root cause of impostor syndrome is a hugely unhelpful picture of what people at the top of society are really like. We feel like impostors, not because we are uniquely flawed but because we can't imagine how deeply flawed the elite must necessarily also be beneath a more or less polished surface.

*

We know ourselves from the inside, but others only from the outside. We're constantly aware of all our anxieties and doubts from within, yet all we know of others is what they happen to do and tell us, a far narrower and more edited source of information. We are very often left to conclude that we must be at the more freakish and revolting end of human nature. We simply don't know others well enough.

*

Everyone is afraid – even those who frighten us.

\*

Feeling lost, making a mess of things, taking longer than seems warranted ... It is all very normal.

\*

No one gets through this life without making dramatic errors. By committing some, we're not proving our wayward nature; we're confirming our membership of the human race.

\*

Any one of us has a theoretical chance of being an agent in history, on a big or small scale. It is open to our own times to build a new city as beautiful as Venice, to change ideas as radically as the Renaissance, to start an intellectual movement as resounding as Buddhism.

\*

We pay others a strange but helpful compliment when we accept them as versions of the same complex and imperfect creatures we know ourselves to be. No one is as strong as they seem – or as daunting as we fear.

*

The present has all the contingency of the past – and is every bit as malleable. How we love, travel, approach the arts, govern, educate ourselves, run businesses, age and die are all up for further development. Current views may appear firm, but only because we exaggerate their fixity.

*

The majority of what exists is arbitary – neither inevitable nor right, simply the result of muddle and happenstance. We should be confident of our power to join the stream of history – and, however modestly, change its course.

*

One of the greatest sources of despair is the belief that things should have been easier than they have in fact turned out to be. We give up, not simply because events are difficult, but because we hadn't expected them to be so. The capacity to remain confident is therefore, to a significant extent, a matter of having internalised a correct narrative about what difficulties are normal to encounter.

\*

We're surrounded by stories of success that conspire to make success seem easier than it in fact is – and therefore that unwittingly destroy the confidence we can muster in the face of our obstacles.

\*

The successful artist or skilled entrepreneur go to great lengths to disguise their labours and make their work appear simple, natural and obvious. 'Art lies in concealing art,' knew the Roman poet Horace. We should, when building anything, keep in mind the agony and struggle behind the art of others.

\*

Confidence isn't the belief that we won't meet obstacles. It is the recognition that difficulties are an inescapable part of all worthwhile contributions.

*

We too easily ignore the most stupid yet deepest fact about our existence: that it will end. The brutal fact of our mortality seems so implausible; we live in practical terms like immortals, as if we will always have the opportunity to address our stifled longings – and thereby lose out on hope, courage and appreciation.

*

By stressing the dangers of failure, we underrate the seriousness of the dangers lurking within passivity. In comparison with the horror of our final exit, the pains and troubles of our bolder moves and riskier ventures do not, in the end, seem so terrifying. We should learn to frighten ourselves a bit more in the area of our mortality, to be less scared of our aspirations.

*

If we saw someone else treating us the way most of us treat ourselves, we might think them despicably cruel.

\*

We cannot change the presence of an enemy, but we can change what an enemy means to us. These figures can shift from being devoted, impartial agents of the truth about one's right to exist to being – more sanely – people who have an opinion, probably only ever a bit right, about something we once said or did, and never about who we are (that is something only we decide).

\*

Memento mori: we need regular, forceful encounters with reminders that there is something else we should be far more frightened of than embarrassment around inviting someone for dinner or starting a new business.

\*

Anyone who deliberately harms us must be a highly damaged and therefore unreliable witness. We should do ourselves the favour of not always thinking too well of our enemies.

\*

When we worry about the verdict of the world, we can remember this analogy from Arthur Schopenhauer: 'Would a musician feel flattered by the loud applause of his audience if it were known to him that, with the exception of one or two, it consisted entirely of deaf people?'

*

Confidence is in large part an internalised version of the confidence that other people once had in us. An inner voice always used to be an outer voice that we have absorbed and made our own.

*

We're so aware of the dangers of self-pity, we overlook the value of calculated moments of self-compassion; we need to appreciate the role of self-care in a good, ambitious and fruitful life.

*

Confidence is, in its essence, entirely compatible with remaining sensitive, kind, witty and softly spoken. It is brutishness, not confidence, we should hate.

*

Being charming is an attempt to neutralise the powerful through their vanity.

\*

5. **Calm**

Whatever their value to science, the sight of the galaxies are in the end as valuable to humankind as counters to megalomania and anxiety.

\*

Social media has taught us a lot about people's deep minds; faith in humanity has ceased to be a realistic option.

\*

There are still people labouring under the unfortunate impression that the best way to cheer someone up is to say something cheerful.

\*

Every failure of calm can be analysed in order to reveal something worth knowing about ourselves. Every worry, frustration, episode of impatience or burst of irritation has significant wisdom to reveal to us, so long as we take the trouble to decode it.

\*

Life is a hospice where we need consolation rather than a hospital where we can hope for a cure.

\*

One or two disasters in a single day can throw one into a black mood. After five or six, matters become almost funny.

\*

Both happiness and misery render us incapable of properly remembering what it was like to experience their converse.

\*

Most visions of happiness blithely assume beating all the statistical odds.

\*

At the end of an average day, our minds are so filled with static, it would take five closely packed pages to begin to capture most of what was fluttering through consciousness.

\*

To despair is to claim to know everything. To decide to kill ourselves is to assume that we are able, from one point in time, to envision the way things will be until the end of our natural days. The only realistic position is to face the future with radical open-mindedness. We can't and don't know what is coming. And therefore a primary reason to carry on is the hope of eventually stumbling on further as yet, for today, unexpected reasons to live. We should banish our despairing surety about what is ahead; the future version of ourselves may look back on who we are right now and beseech us silently to keep faith with the journey. We can't know from here about the years to come and, for that reason alone, must give ourselves every generous chance to find out.

*

Things only ever seem stable because we aren't standing close enough to them to realise their contingency.

*

Planetariums can seem as if they are trying to show us the stars in order to equip us with the knowledge required to one day become astronauts or physicists. In truth, they offer us a means with which to diminish ourselves in our own eyes; they are a tool with which to take the sting out of our nagging sense of unimportance and our frustration at our modest achievements and sense of isolation.

*

To every reversal, we should simply answer that there are 40 billion planetary systems at large in the universe. Before every anxiety-inducing date or speech, we should mutter to ourselves, like a talismanic prayer, that the Milky Way is 100,000 light years across and that the most distant known galaxy is GN-z11, 32 billion light years from the restaurant or conference centre.

*

Growing up should mean feeling ever less unique – in painful and redemptive ways.

*

The true scale of things keeps escaping us – the age of the earth and the size of the universe, of course. But closer to home, just how many people there are on the planet, how varied their lives are, how dense the stories, how varied the destinies … We wildly exaggerate what is close to us, how representative and significant it is. We need a sign in our eyesight at all times; we are operating with the wrong perspective.

\*

When we are ill, we want people to be as caring as if we were dying – but as robustly reassuring as if we were immortal.

\*

We can never properly be secure, because so long as we are alive, we will be at risk in some way. The only people with full security are the dead; the only people who can be truly at peace are under the ground; cemeteries are the only definitively calm places around.

\*

Insomnia is the mind's revenge for all the thoughts we carefully forgot to have in the day.

*

Addiction is the manic reliance on something, anything, to keep our darker or more unsettling thoughts and feelings at bay. What properly indicates addiction is not *what* someone is addicted to, for we can get addicted to pretty much anything (news, exercise, heroin). It is the motives behind a reliance on a certain element – and, in particular, our attachment to it as a way of avoiding encounters with the contents of our own minds and hearts.

*

We typically think of anger as a dark and pessimistic state of mind, but behind anger lies a surprising emotion: optimism. The angry are, beneath their ranting, possessed of some recklessly optimistic notions of how life might go. They are not merely in a destructive fury; they are in the grip of hope.

*

We should spare ourselves the burden of loneliness; everyone is more anxious than they are inclined to tell us. We've collectively failed to admit to ourselves what we are truly like.

*

The person who shouts every time they encounter a traffic jam betrays a faith, at once touching and demented, that roads must always be (mysteriously) traffic-free. The person who loses their temper with every new employee, child or partner evinces a curious belief that perfection is an option for the human animal.

*

Anxiety is not always a sign of sickness, a weakness of the mind or an error to which we should locate a medical solution. It is mostly a hugely reasonable and sensitive response to the genuine strangeness, terror, uncertainty and riskiness of existence.

*

We must learn to laugh about our anxieties – laughter being the exuberant expression of relief when a hitherto private agony is given a well-crafted social formulation in a joke. We must suffer alone. But we can at least hold out our arms to our similarly tortured, fractured, and, above all else, anxious neighbours, as if to say, in the kindest way possible, 'I know …'

*

Once we have acquired the skill of cheerful despair, a new range of possibilities for pleasure opens itself up to us. We will be amazed and so touched when, once in a while, someone seems to understand a few things we mean. We will take note, with some astonishment, that not everyone has plans to murder or hurt others. We will make the most of the constrained but real opportunities we have. We will be free to enjoy the distinctive cheerful despair of those who have taken every fateful fact about life on board.

*

Not everything that makes us *sad* makes us *angry*. We may be irritated that it is raining, but we are unlikely ever to respond to a shower by screaming. We aren't overwhelmed by anger whenever we are frustrated; we are sent into a rage only when we first allow ourselves to believe in a hopeful scenario that is then dashed suddenly and apparently without warning. Our greatest furies spring from unfortunate events that we have not factored into our vision of reality.

*

Modernity never ceases to emphasise that success could, somehow, one day be ours. And in this way, it never ceases to (gently) torture us.

*

Reflect on how little we care about most others, even those we know quite well: we don't have much of a handle on what they do; we can't recall how they got on with their siblings; we forget their greatest regrets – and it doesn't always seem overly important to find out. There is no ill will, just a natural deep lack of curiosity. They are not thinking much about us, or we about them.

*

Everything that happens to us, or that we do, is of no consequence whatsoever from the point of view of Enceladus, the sixth largest moon of Saturn.

*

A single storm raged on Saturn from December 2010 to September 2011; at its peak the winds gusted for hundreds of thousands of kilometres, encircling the entire planet.

*

In 1775 BCE, Zimri-Lin was King of Mari, a city on the banks of the Euphrates. He was one of the most glamorous, wealthy and powerful individuals of his century. He is now remembered by a small fragment of a wall painting in which he is depicted standing next to a cow.

*

Sit alone in the kitchen and try to imagine what our planet looks like from the perspective of the star Deneb, located in the constellation of Cygnus, 1,550 light years away from earth.

*

To exaggerate despair so wildly – until one remembers there might yet be a few things to live for.

*

Behind every anxiety lies a hope of success; calm is the reward for throttling ambition.

*

There is no such thing as work–life balance. Everything worth fighting for unbalances your life.

*

The best way to release oneself from the grip of an anxiety is to spend so long on it, to discuss it so much with so many people that – eventually – one has a chance to evade it through ... boredom.

*

The upside of catastrophism: a string of pleasant surprises.

*

There is, curiously, a persistent relief to be found in the knowledge of the inevitability of suffering. It is, in the end, not darkness that dooms us but the wrong sort of hope.

*

Melancholy is not rage or bitterness; it is a noble species of sadness that arises when we are open to the fact that life is inherently difficult for everyone and that suffering and disappointment are at the heart of human experience. It is not a disorder that needs to be cured; it is a tender-hearted, calm, dispassionate acknowledgement of how much pain we must inevitably all travel through.

*

The melancholy person lacks any of the bitter one's original optimism and therefore has no need to respond to disappointments with a resentful or wounded gnarl. They understood from an early age that most of life would be boredom and agony and structured their worldview accordingly. They aren't of course delighted by the mess and the insults, the meanness and the hardship, but nor can they muster the energy to believe that it was really meant to be any other way.

*

Melancholy links pain with wisdom and beauty. It springs from a rightful awareness of the tragic structure of every life. We can, in melancholy states, understand without fury or sentimentality, that no one truly understands anyone else, that loneliness is universal and that every life has its full measure of shame and sorrow. The wisdom of the melancholy attitude lies in the understanding that we have not been singled out, that our suffering belongs to humanity in general. Melancholy is marked by an impersonal take on suffering. It is filled with pity for the human condition.

*

We need not feel ashamed at our despair; it's simply an inevitable part of being alive. Whatever is sometimes implied, it is normal, very normal, to be in agony. We don't, on top of it all, need to be brave.

*

Almost all of us end up drinking equal amounts from the cup of human sorrow – just at different points, in different sized sips.

*

So many of life's complaints boil down to the belly ache of the fragile, mortal, ignored ego taking stock of its place in a vast and indifferent universe.

\*

# 6. Leisure

We may try to blame our lack of creative inspiration on not being sufficiently 'well read' – yet how vastly better read we already are, by simple virtue of the times we live in, than Plato, the Buddha or Shakespeare.

\*

Newspapers are to the real complexity of a nation as the icons in weather forecasts are to the subtleties of the sky.

\*

The secret hope on picking up a book: that it will tell us what we already feel but haven't had time to think.

\*

With time and many upheavals, it's the quiet 'boring' days with nothing planned that start to feel like the truly exciting ones.

\*

However resigned or lonely we might be, it's always hard to pass through airport Arrivals on one's own without an irrational hope that someone significant has come along to surprise us after all.

\*

Aphorisms: provocative, exaggerated sentences that overstate their case as a way of flushing out an occasional truth.

*

The reason to travel: there are inner transitions we can't properly cement without a change of location.

*

Being funny should only ever be an incidental by-product of trying to get to an important truth, never a destination in itself.

*

Their defenders have to accept that the finest works of art can usually do less for us than a siesta or an aspirin.

*

We get angry with talented writers who have refused to write precisely the books we can't extract from our own unconscious.

*

Embarking on another book, writers seldom dare note that few of their favourite authors ever wrote more than two or three works they really loved.

*

You have to be bashed about a bit by life to see the point of flowers, pretty skies and uneventful 'boring' days.

*

The more we understand what reading is for us, the more we can enjoy intimate relationships with a few works only. Our libraries can be small. Re-reading might become crucial; we'll pay attention to the reinforcement of what we already know but tend so often to forget. The truly well-read person isn't the one who has read a gargantuan number of books; it's someone who has let themselves be shaped – in their capacity to live and die well – by a very few well-chosen titles.

*

Good books put a finger on emotions that are deeply our own – but that we could never have described on our own.

*

Whatever the charms of an author with whose views we concur perfectly, nothing can quite beat the service sometimes paid to us by someone who we feel is tantalisingly off tangent, an author who starts to say something interesting, but then (in our eyes) goes resolutely off piste, an author who hovers close to an essential point but then drops it in favour of something maddeningly trivial, misguided or irrelevant. Assisted by the author's ploughing of the intellectual landscape, our personal thoughts can start to germinate in deeply authentic and vivid directions. We put down the book and find a whole portion of our own thinking revealed to us. Our argument with the author powers our own reflections. By not saying what we quite wished to hear, the author brings us into newfound contact with what we actually believe, and does us the immense service of releasing us from our intellectual underconfidence and languor.

*

The role of books in reminding us of what we think through our inner arguments with them changes our sense of what an ideal curriculum might look like. It may include the sensible masterpieces, of course, but there is all the more reason to find space in it for all the books that are fruitfully not very good or fascinatingly misconstrued or inspiringly erratic. So-called 'bad' books might, when considered as a tool for thinking, be just as effective as the acknowledged good ones – and sometimes a lot better – for, as we turn their pages, they allow us secretly to imagine our own superior versions of what we are taking in.

\*

One kind of good book should leave us asking, 'How did the author know that about me?'

\*

Boredom has many important things to teach us. It is, at its best, a confused, inarticulate but genuine signal from a deep part of our minds that something is very wrong. We may not quite know what but the sensation of being bored frequently contains (especially for otherwise sensible adults) an apprehension of genuine danger. There are boring books that should – with real fairness – be tossed aside. There are boring people we should, in order not to wither inside, refuse to see. There are boring films we should walk out of. And what should sharpen our courage to do so is an ongoing awareness that the fundamental currency of our lives is time, of which we are in desperately short supply, there being on average no more than 26,000 days or so in an entire existence on the planet.

*

Religions are intermittently too creative, interesting and useful to be abandoned merely to those who happen to believe in them. The priority is to rescue some of what is still wise, inspiring and relevant from all that is no longer true.

*

It is sensible enough to try to live longer lives. But we are working with a false notion of what long really means. We might live to be a thousand years old and still complain that it had all rushed by too fast. We should be aiming to lead lives that feel long because we have managed to imbue them with the right sort of open-hearted appreciation and unsnobbish receptivity, the kind that five-year-olds know naturally how to bring to bear. We don't need to add years; we need to densify the time we have left by ensuring that every day is lived consciously – and we can do this via a manoeuvre as simple as it is momentous: by starting to notice all that we have as yet only seen.

\*

At its best, art is a tool that reminds us of how little we have fathomed and noticed. It re-introduces us to ordinary things and reopens our eyes to a latent beauty and interest in precisely those areas we had ceased to bother with. It helps us to recover some of the manic sensitivity we had as newborns.

\*

The best but hardest way to diet: ensure that one has more nourishing things to do than eat.

*

It feels counter-intuitive to insist that there might be many things more important than the news. But there is: our own lives – which the news has, troublingly in modern society, been granted such prestigious reasons to suggest that we should avoid studying in its name.

*

There is great joy in turning upsets into theories and one boring and frustrating dinner into an aphorism that can last.

*

It's a measure of how much a bit of our mind hates us to hatch and be disturbed by new thoughts that we have to write them down immediately to have any chance of holding on to them. Most of the mind far favours ease over insight.

*

It is extremely rare to properly delight in flowers when one is under twenty-two; it is rare to be left entirely indifferent by flowers after the age of fifty. One will have been fully inducted into the extent of human wickedness and folly – and to one's own eccentricity, selfishness and madness. And so, by then, flowers will have started to seem somewhat different – no longer a petty distraction from a mighty destiny, no longer an insult to ambition, but a genuine pleasure amidst a litany of troubles.

*

The destiny of every properly good idea is to be popular, and so the task of good thinking must include not just the formulation of good ideas but also their powerful and seductive dissemination.

*

Often, we start crying at films, not when things are horrible but when they are suddenly and unexpectedly precisely the opposite, when they are unusually sweet, tender, joyful, innocent or kind. Weeping in such circumstances is telling us something important: it's a sign of how hard our lives have become.

*

It should not only be children who go to school. All adults should see themselves as in need of education pretty much every day. One should never be done with school. One should stay an active alumni, learning throughout life. Schools should be where a community gets educated, not just a place for children. Some classes should have seven-year-olds learning alongside fifty-year-olds (the two cohorts having been found to have equivalent maturities in a given area). In the utopia, the phrase 'I've finished school' would sound extremely strange.

*

It is a tribute to both art and religion to suggest that culture should now replace the role in society once held by scripture.

*

It is books, poems, paintings that often give us the confidence to take seriously feelings in ourselves that we might otherwise never have thought to acknowledge.

*

'A book (though the same could be said of any art form) must be the axe for the frozen sea inside us,' proposed Kafka – in other words, a tool to help release us from our numbness, to allow us to shed tears and to provide occasions for catharsis in areas where we have for too long been damagingly brave.

*

The best books help us to rediscover the exiled bits of ourselves.

*

A good life requires us to do two relatively tricky things: know how to go along with the rules sufficiently well so as not to get mired in needless fights with the school authorities and, simultaneously, never to believe too blindly or too passively in the long-term validity of everything we're asked to study. We need to be outwardly obedient and inwardly discerning.

*

What we call 'beautiful' is any work of art that supplies a missing dose of a much-needed psychological component, and we dismiss as 'ugly' one that forces on us moods or motifs that we feel threatened or already overwhelmed by. Our contact with art holds out the promise of inner wholeness.

\*

It is very rare to find a thoughtful adult who – by middle age or earlier – does not, at certain moments of crisis, look back in a somewhat puzzled way at their school years and wonder why, amidst all the study, the discipline and the earnest commitment, so much managed to be passed over in silence. How come, in all those hours sitting in classrooms, did certain fundamental concepts that would have been so important to a half-way decent life slip through the net? How come there was so much time for calculus, the erosion of the upper glacial layer, the politics of the Burgundian states of the 1400s, the poetry of Emily Dickinson and trigonometric equations, and yet so little time for a range of puzzles that have rendered grown-up life so tricky? Why – in short – did no one ever tell us?

\*

Journeys can be the midwives of our best, more creative thoughts.

*

A capacity to appreciate life's small moments is related to an underlying darker sense that the whole can never be made perfect.

*

Though it may feel otherwise, enjoying life is no more dangerous than apprehending it with continuous anxiety and gloom.

*

Because life itself so often seems incomprehensible, books that one can hardly understand may seem closer to the mark than those one can understand.

*

Most of what makes a book 'good' is that we're reading it at the right moment for us.

*

Cooks make the food others are too busy to prepare. Writers articulate the thoughts others are too preoccupied to formulate.

*

It's not perfect that people should be merely pretending to be cultured. But how pleasant that they're bothering to fake matters in that direction.

*

There is the laughter that comes not when one has never really cried but when one has cried for years, when every pretty hope has been trampled on, when one has made some properly dreadful mistakes and been repaid amply for them – and when one has fully considered ending it all, but then decided – at the last moment – to keep going, not because of anything one can expect of oneself, not because one holds on to any standard belief in a good life, but because – amidst the shitshow – one can't help but notice that the sky is a delightful azure blue, that there's a Bach cello concerto to listen to and that there's a sweet four-year-old holding on to her mother's hand, asking how ducks sleep at night. And so, despite everything, the loneliness, the shame, the compromise, the self-hatred and the sure knowledge that the agony isn't over yet, one turns to the light and says a big rebellious obstinate joyful yes to the universe (which naturally doesn't give a damn).

*

# 7. Others

What need is there to weep over parts of life? The whole of it calls for tears.

– *Seneca (c. 4 BCE–65 CE)*

＊

On the highest throne in the world, we are seated, still, upon our arses.

– *Montaigne (1533–1592)*

＊

Kings and philosophers shit, and so do ladies.

– *Montaigne (1533–1592)*

＊

To learn that we have said or done a stupid thing is nothing; we must learn a more ample and important lesson: that we are but blockheads.

– *Montaigne (1533–1592)*

＊

No man is a hero to his valet.

– *Montaigne (1533–1592)*

＊

All of humanity's problems stem from man's inability to sit quietly in a room alone.
– Pascal (1623–1662)

*

Anyone who does not see the vanity of the world is very vain himself.
– Pascal (1623–1662)

*

Man's greatness comes from knowing he is wretched.
– Pascal (1623–1662)

*

We all have strength enough to bear the misfortunes of others.
– La Rochefoucauld (1613–1680)

*

To boast that one never flirts is actually a kind of flirtation.
– La Rochefoucauld (1613–1680)

*

There are some people who would never have fallen in love if they hadn't heard there was such a thing.
– *La Rochefoucauld (1613–1680)*

*

A man should swallow a toad every day to be sure of not meeting with anything more disgusting in the day ahead.
– *Chamfort (1741–1794)*

*

It is sometimes said of a man who lives alone that he does not like society. This is like saying of a man that he does not like going for walks because he is not fond of walking at night in the forêt de Bondy.
– *Chamfort (1741–1794)*

*

To understand a man you have to know what was happening in the world when he was twenty.
– *Napoleon (1769–1821)*

*

Today it is bad, and day by day it will get worse – until at last the worst of all happens.
– *Schopenhauer (1788–1860)*

\*

Human life must be some kind of mistake.
– *Schopenhauer (1788–1860)*

\*

After his fortieth year, any man of merit ... will hardly be free from a certain touch of misanthropy.
– *Schopenhauer (1788–1860)*

\*

In the minds of geniuses, we find – once more – our own neglected thoughts.
– *Ralph Waldo Emerson (1803–1882)*

\*

Marry, and you will regret it; don't marry, you will also regret it; marry or don't marry, you will regret it either way. Laugh at the world's foolishness, you will regret it; weep over it, you will regret that too; laugh at the world's foolishness or weep over it, you will regret both. Believe a woman, you will regret it; believe her not, you will also regret it ... Hang yourself, you will regret it; do not hang yourself, and you will regret that too; hang yourself or don't hang yourself, you'll regret it either way; whether you hang yourself or do not hang yourself, you will regret both. This, gentlemen, is the essence of all philosophy.

– *Søren Kierkegaard (1813–1855)*

\*

If we had a keen vision and feeling of all ordinary human life, it would be like hearing the grass grow and the squirrel's heart beat, and we should die of that roar which lies on the other side of silence.

– *George Eliot (1819–1880)*

\*

When we are tired, we are attacked by ideas we conquered long ago.
– *Friedrich Nietzsche (1844–1900)*

\*

When two people part, it is the one who is not in love who makes the tender speeches.
– *Marcel Proust (1871–1922)*

\*

The catastrophe you fear will happen has already happened.
– *Donald Winnicott (1896–1971)*

\*

**The School of Life** publishes a range of books on essential topics in psychological and emotional life, including relationships, parenting, friendship, careers and fulfilment. The aim is always to help us to understand ourselves better – and thereby to grow calmer, less confused and more purposeful. Discover our full range of titles, including books for children, here:

www.theschooloflife.com/books

**The School of Life** also offers a comprehensive therapy service, which complements, and draws upon, our published works:

www.theschooloflife.com/therapy